UNDER CONSTRUCTION

Navigating the Detours on the Road to Recovery

Dug McGuirk

Health Communications, Inc.
Deerfield Beach, Florida

www.hcibooks.com

Library of Congress Cataloging-in-Publication Data
is available through the Library of Congress

©2019 Dug McGuirk

ISBN-13: 978-07573-2033-0 (Paperback)
ISBN-10: 07573-2033-3 (Paperback)
ISBN-13: 978-07573-2034-7 (ePub)
ISBN-10: 07573-2034-1 (ePub)

All rights reserved. Printed in the United States of America. No part of this publication may be reproduced, stored in a retrieval system, or transmitted in any form or by any means, electronic, mechanical, photocopying, recording, or otherwise, without the written permission of the publisher.

HCI, its logos, and marks are trademarks of Health Communications, Inc.

Publisher: Health Communications, Inc.
 3201 S.W. 15th Street
 Deerfield Beach, FL 33442–8190

Cover design by Larissa Hise Henoch
Interior design and formatting by Lawna Patterson Oldfield

This book is first and foremost dedicated to my incredible wife Heidi Rain and our most amazing gift, our daughter Ellovie Rain; I am eternally grateful for our life together. Without Heidi's love, support, and inspiration, I would certainly not be who I am today. Relentless in her pursuit of growth and in her contribution of energy and ideas, Heidi is a true role model to everyone who knows her—including our little girl, Ellie.

Heidi and I were blessed to work together for a number of years in the drug and alcohol treatment field where we designed special programs for people struggling with addictions and their families. Working together enabled us to learn so much about ourselves, each other, and our clients. Seeing them heal, grow, and pay it forward is just about as fulfilling and heartening as it gets for us. If you are not familiar with Heidi's work or haven't had the chance to participate in any of her programs, check them out at *RevelutionaryGrowth.com*.

This book is also dedicated to you, dear reader. The world needs you. Your family and friends need you. When you learn to access all of your dormant power and energy, you will enjoy a life liberated from the things that have slowed you down or muted your divine light. By reading this, you are giving yourself a wonderful gift—an opportunity for true transformation and a life of happiness. I am humbled by your spirit of willingness—I believe in you and your ability to change. Love yourself for who you are *and* who you aren't—I do!

Contents

Preface vii

Introduction: The Bad Drive 1

CHAPTER 1: **Emotion Is Fuel** 7

CHAPTER 2: **The Behavioral Trinity** 29

CHAPTER 3: **The Four Tiers of Human Experience** 59

CHAPTER 4: **The Six Human Needs** 67

CHAPTER 5: **Gassing Up for the Trip** 85

CHAPTER 6: **Rules of the Road** 109

True Story: Manifestation Proxy 127

About Dug McGuirk: Revolutionary Growth 133

Preface

I really want to acknowledge you for the journey you're on and for taking an interest in this book. We all have busy lives and face many challenges, but the fact that you're here letting me share your journey speaks incredible volumes about how committed you are to creating a better life.

This book—this time—is for you and your loved ones because whatever you do—positive or negative—you are still going to be in those relationships, and whatever you do will impact them, too. By reading this book and applying the principles, you will be better equipped to be the best you can be for yourself and, therefore, the best you can be for them—your parents, spouse, sweetheart, or children. You're going to restore the part of that great connection that you once had.

If you are in recovery, that's a big part of your (and their) life transformation. Recovery—do you know what that word means? You can probably guess just by parsing the word re-cover: to go back to the individual, the return of something that has been lost. Now the way you were is what got you here in the first place. But we're going to celebrate what is working for you, not beat you up over all the things that aren't—you're great at doing that on your own. We're going to refocus on what's great in your life, then add what's missing—reawaken the parts of you that have become dormant.

Isn't it true that over time, parts of you have lost their luster? How often do you say things like, "When I was a kid, I used to have so much fun doing this or that, now it's not very much fun anymore?" This book will help you change all of that so that when you're done, you will have had a few "aha!" moments where you'll say things like, "aha! I get it now!" Two of the mantras you will hear throughout this book, so you might as well learn them now, are: *using drugs or alcohol was not a problem, it was the solution* and *nothing has any meaning except the meaning you give it*. You're going to discover why they are so important and how to step over those road bumps.

WELCOME TO YOUR REVOLUTION!

Let's start with a story about a turkey . . .

This is a story about a turkey and a little girl named Sally. It's Christmastime and Sally and her mom are in the kitchen preparing the holiday dinner. Sally is five years old now and ready to learn to cook—especially the Christmas turkey! Sally is so excited—this means she's growing up because, wow, making the Christmas turkey is a really big deal! Sally helps mom get all the ingredients out and the old recipe card that has been passed down for generations.

The first thing mom does is set the turkey in the pan and cut the legs off—the first thing Sally does is ask questions (as kids do). "Mom, why'd you just do that?" she asks. Mom thinks about it and tells Sally, 'I don't know—it's the way grandma taught me. Let's ask her." So they call up Grandma and Sally asks, "Grandma, Grandma! I'm making the turkey and mommy cut the legs off like you, do but she doesn't know why!" And Grandma says, "I don't know, that's the way my mom taught me. I'll ask her." Now great-grandma is rather old but still kicking and adding tons of love and value to the family. Grandma calls her and asks, "Mama, why do we cut the legs off the Christmas turkey?" The old matriarch thought about it for a moment and began laughing so hard she that she's gasping for breath. Great-grandma is just cracking up laughing until grandma asks her what's so funny. "Oh, my goodness!" she said, "Back when I learned how to cook a turkey the ovens were so small that you couldn't fit a whole one in the oven so I cut the legs off so it would fit!"

Now before we really get going, I'm asking you to question where you learned how to do some things. Whose turkey are you cooking these days? That goes for your loved ones, too—whose turkey are they cooking? Where did they learn to do that?

When we label someone an addict, we're going back to an old tradition. At the time, they thought it was helpful, so the practice stuck. Is it always (or ever) appropriate? We'll check the ecology in the chapters ahead and consistently ask what something means.

If I say, "Hi, I'm Kerry and I'm an addict," does it means that I'm broken, that something is wrong with me? Does it mean that I'm the dirt of society? When an addict uses it, they are acknowledging that they have a problem and that they feel badly about it. Do they use it as an excuse? Sometimes they do. But if it means they're managing their problem daily and celebrating the fact that they're overcoming it, that's a different label all together. The ecology works out, it's just a different question with a very different meaning.

Does the ID—the label you give something—serve a bigger picture ecologically? Does it serve your loved ones? Does it serve who you truly are and support your transformation? You have to answer the question! Now, if I say, "Hi, I'm Kerry, I'm an addict," your response should be, "No... that's just a label, who *else* are you?" Start an awakening! The things I share with you in this book mean nothing when I tell them to you, but if you tell yourself, they mean *everything!*

Be careful how you label yourself—be true—learn and grow from these ideas but make them your own—tell yourself so you really believe them! And remember that *nothing has any meaning except the meaning you give it.*

Introduction: The Bad Drive

Like millions of people on planet Earth, I've had my share of turbulent times. And like most of them, I've survived, black eyes and bruised egos notwithstanding. But I've learned a thing or two along the way that changed my life in very specific ways that are unique to my own personal journey—life-changing things that I'm eager to share with you. Those life experiences brought me to the place where I am today and fashioned the person who I am today. Many years ago, I decided that I would spend the rest of my life discovering, growing, and sharing things I've learned to help others facing their own challenging times. With seemingly insurmountable odds now in my rearview mirror, I've been able to put those experiences in proper perspective and focus on the future. With hindsight as an indispensable teacher, I set a course for a new path as a therapist, mentor, speaker, and workshop facilitator, helping others pick up the pieces of their lives and glue them back together in beautiful, complicated mosaics.

The title of this book is *Under Construction: Navigating the Road to Recovery* because that's how life is—it's never truly finished with us until we reach the end of the road. Metaphorically, the term "under construction" represents the way life seems to present itself as we work our way through it.

Imagine for a moment that you are driving your car on a clear day. You have a full tank of gas, your passengers are comfortable, the radio is playing your favorite songs, and the ride feels great. Then, out of nowhere, dark clouds blanket the sky overhead. Within seconds, the pitter-patter of falling rain interrupts the rhythm of the music. Your phone rings—it's your mother calling with her usual drama and trauma (and some that aren't even hers). Before long, the drops of rain turn into a torrential downpour and your wipers can't keep up. Just a few minutes ago, what was a clear, open road is now full of traffic with large trucks and vans in every lane pushing along at different speeds and blocking your view to the way ahead. As heavy thunderclouds obscure a sunny sky, headlights blink on one by one and you're blinded by the oncoming traffic. As the wheels of a semi spray oily grey mud onto your windshield and the radio turns to static, one of your friends in the backseat asks a question that beckons a thoughtful answer. Moving inch by inch, you're doing your best to concentrate on the road and respond to the question with compassion and sincerity, when you notice a sign reading "Detour Ahead." Before you can process your limited options, you hit a pothole and your thoughts shift to flat tires and dented rims as the fuel light flashes red. You idle precariously in the parking lot that moments ago was a wide-open highway and you imagine the car sputtering and stalling and the cost of new tires and alignment. While all this is going on, you look for signs beyond the vague "Detour Ahead" to get you back en route because now your GPS is no longer reliable. Frustrated, you realize that your journey is going to get even more complicated because you have absolutely no directions for this unexpected path and your passengers from out of town have no clue how to help. Now that you are dealing with multiple obstacles and challenges at the same time, I ask you: How effective at addressing any or all of these obstacles can you possibly be?

Think back on a time when you or someone you care about experienced this level of upheaval. How much compassion did you have for yourself or your loved one during that time? Can you look back now at that experience with empathy and love and forgive yourself, knowing that you did the best you could? Have you come out from under the ordeal with new wisdom, access to grace and elegance, and new confidence to support and overcome future challenges?

This driving metaphor describes the emotional, psychological, and physical upheavals you and I go through as we navigate our way along the road of life. No doubt, at some point in your life, you have had similar experiences or you know someone who has. In hindsight, as I was chin-deep in the sludge, I was not a very effective leader or visionary, but today I am capable of handling those experiences in a very different manner. When you are mired in upheavals, it can be almost impossible to differentiate the picture from the frame, but with some dissociated distance, you can gain perspective from, and appreciation for, those experiences, including the difficulties we put other people through, too. Think back on a time when you or a friend seemed to have a string of bad luck that just never seemed to end. How did you cope? How did you navigate your way through? At those times, real compassion is your most valuable resource and you will find that a small shift in focus and change of questions becomes power. You can't expect yourself or others to function normally, no less at peak state, with all that craziness going on. But, simply acknowledging the challenges stacking up in your path can open up a world of possibilities—open roads, blue skies, potholes, and detours—a world you will learn to navigate with confidence.

During my eventful journey down some of these twisting roads, I have had the great fortune of discovering and accessing an array of useful tools that have helped me navigate many challenges. Some of them I learned by studying personal development through total immersion in the field: I became a Master Practitioner and Trainer of Neurolinguistics Programming (NLP) and Neo-Erickson Hypnosis. I spent over four years working with a world leader in self-development, Tony Robbins, with whom I traveled the country as a speaker and trainer, managing between two and four sessions a day. At the time of this writing, I spent the last six years at one of the country's leading addiction treatment centers, guiding people through the difficult process of recovery (having overcome my own addiction at a very young age, the field of recovery is very close to my heart). I have coached, taught, and spoken at conferences on addiction and recovery across the country; it is this experience and confidence that is both the impetus and the backbone of this book. It's important to note, however, that the philosophies I share in *Under Construction* are not exclusive to substance abuse at all. In fact, you will find that these perspectives support recovery from any thought or behavior pattern that keeps you from creating the life of your dreams. One of the guiding principles I will show you relative to substance abuse is that drugs and alcohol are not the problem. As a matter of fact, they have always been the solution. They are an effective vehicle we can choose to use, but they are not sustainable and, if not addressed, they can become a problem. Or, as you will also learn, they can become an opportunity.

Under Construction will also help you understand why I believe that not only can we successfully arrive at a desired destination, but equally important, we can truly enjoy the journey! Now here's what I want you to do: As you read this book, give yourself a gift—put aside all the things you "know" or you "think" you know, and allow yourself the joy of curiosity. If you let them, the concepts I share with you in this book can influence and enhance your own perspectives. Plus, reading this book should be easy and fun—you've already showed initiative by picking it up, and you've already invested time by reading this far.

We are kindred spirits; let's try out a new car or truck or motorcycle together—whatever you would like to drive down this road. Let's get a fresh tank of premium gas, change the oil, put on some new tires, and get our windows super-clean (after all, that's how you started out on this journey). By the end of this book, it's my hope that you will realize that everything you need to be successful is already within you. It really doesn't matter *what* you drive, it's *how* you drive, and I'm going to prove that you have the power and capability to own the road—to live the life you really want. The obstacles and detours are no easier in one car than another—it all comes down to how you navigate your way through and around them. You've heard the line before: life is a journey. When you accept that you are special and unique and that you have something valuable to offer, you're going to have a very different trip. You're going to go places!

CHAPTER 1

Emotion Is Fuel

THE THREE PILLARS OF TRANSFORMATION

Let's start our road trip at the beginning, with the *Three Pillars of Transformation*: State, Strategy, and Story. It's important that we begin by filling up with the right fuel to make the journey smooth and enjoyable.

State

What is State and why is it so important? It's your state of mind, your state of being, your emotional state, or simply, how you feel—your emotional fuel. Imagine that you have a new car and you want to go somewhere. If you could go anywhere you want, where would you like to go? Most of us immediately choose a destination that we associate with pleasure—the beach, the mountains, a spa, or grandma's house. For now, let's say you want to go to the bank. Why would you want go to there? Because you want to "fuel up"—you want to get money to buy things or have experiences that will make you feel good. Somewhere in your blueprint it is written that you need things to feel full, complete, or happy. It's what drives you—what drives us all—to acquire things and experiences that we think will make us feel good. We have been taught that in order to drive with our tank full of positive emotions, we first need to satisfy that desire. Now, what if I told you that you've been fueling up the wrong way your entire life? What if you could find an infinite supply of clean, high-efficiency fuel to run on? Would you make the switch? Of course you would, and I'll show you exactly how to make that happen.

Let's look at it this way: think of your favorite gas-powered car, your dream car. Imagine sitting in the driver's seat of this incredible car, gripping the steering wheel with both hands. You start it up and realize that the gas tank is almost empty. Do you drive the high-performance car of your dreams to the nearest gas station—Steve's Thrift Shop, Bait & Tackle, that also happens to sell 84-octane—and fill up? Would you risk putting bottom-of-the-barrel gasoline in the engine of your dream car? Of course not. If you did, what kind of performance would you expect to get? Suboptimal fuel will give you suboptimal performance: crappy gas will yield crappy results. On top of that, you risk damaging the engine of your beloved car. So it is when you act out of fear, anger, resentment, or any other negative or non-resourceful, lesser grade emotion—it is the equivalent of driving your super cool car on super poor gasoline. You wouldn't think of doing that to one of your most prized possessions, so why would you do it to your life? Why would you fill up on poor quality States or emotions? It simply doesn't make sense, but some of us do it every day.

Let's go back to why we want money. When it comes down to it, you and I don't really want money per se, we want what money can do for us—we want what it will buy and how we think it will make us feel. We don't want to buy things just to have things, we want what those things will do to our mood or State. We really just want to feel good. Inherently, you and I know that we make better decisions with better outcomes when we are in better States. For instance, here is a question I often ask clients and participants at my events: Have you ever made a bad decision? Without fail, hands go up in assent. But a decision is simply a decision, that's all. The outcome of your decision may not be what you would like or expect, yet in the end, it's just a decision. What needs to be addressed is not our decision-making ability, it's the emotional state we are in when making decisions. Negative States (fuel) will generate negative outcomes.

Now that we've made this distinction, it's time to become familiar with your Emotional Guidance System—your EGS—which is basically a GPS that shows you the way to go. In the example above, the bank and money were not actually the destination—changing to a positive State was the true destination. Once you know that, you can set your EGS accordingly and reach your destination with much more ease and confidence.

Ultimately, feeling great is your desired State—your desired emotional fuel. What if you entered a destination into your EGS and it told you there was an alternate, much shorter route to get there? And what if it told you that there was a gas station a few minutes away where you could fill your tank with all the clean, high-grade "feel good" you need? If your positive emotions tank is full, then you could enjoy your entire ride from the very beginning and even choose different destinations. If your tank is full of happiness and passion, then you don't need to go to the bank to get money and buy things like a high to feel amazing. Perhaps you'd spend time with friends or loved ones instead, or work on some of those projects you've been putting off, because now that you feel great, they no longer seem like chores. Yet, millions of us drive around most of our lives trying to escape the things that are important to us because we can't find a way to derive pleasure from them. As a result, once we realize that we haven't done the things we meant to do, we end up feeling guilty, unfulfilled, empty.

Earlier on I said that you've been fueling up the wrong way. Well, fueling up the right way is exactly what successful people are experts at doing. By successful, I mean people who are hitting the mark in all areas of life—they are happy and wealthy in their energy, relationships, work, and, best of all, their spirit. They are familiar with the infinite, clean, high-grade fuel we've been talking about, and the first thing they do every day of their lives is fill up with it. They start out feeling great instead of taking long drives only to feel great at the end. Remember this chain of thought because we're going to discuss it more down the road when we get to the tiers of experience that create sustainability.

Where do successful people get their fuel? How do they generate their desired States? Every day they prime their pump and fill their tank by creating their own emotion fuel. They become so good at it that they enjoy the entire ride while focusing on new challenges and reaching new destinations at the same time. Successful people value a life well-lived and they value happiness to such a degree that they create their own joy. They know that money and things won't make them feel great, yet by feeling great it becomes easier for them to do the necessary things to create money, to buy things and experiences. They're using the right fuel and heading for the right destination. What you and I need to do is learn how to prime our pumps with the proper fuel, too, in order to get to our true destination. Have you ever siphoned gas out of one container into another? Do you know how a siphon works? I'll explain how this concept applies to our emotional fuel or State just ahead.

In the meantime, let's shift our focus a little. What are drugs and alcohol? Why do people use them? They take drugs and drink alcohol because they are quick ways to change their State and to feel good. These substances become part of their strategy to change how they feel in relation to their EGS. Millions of people sit around every day waiting to win an emotional lottery. They don't get it. There is no such thing. Using drugs and alcohol is like swiping an emotional and spiritual credit card—the happiness is not real, and eventually, it has to be paid back. Have you ever put yourself into emotional debt that way? You use, go into debt, then you feel worse. You swipe again. When that card is maxed-out, you take another one and keep swiping. You continue swiping until, finally, you can't get another credit card. Now you've ended up in a different kind of State—a state of desperation. Why do people do that? Well, to get to the truth, we need to understand some of the science behind the behavior. First and foremost, we are wired to feel pain. Neurobiologically speaking, our pain sensors outnumber our pleasure sensors by a ratio of 10:1. That means our natural inclination is to not only *notice* pain and discomfort, but to *do something* about it. Action is the antidote, but it can create a vicious cycle: we take action to avoid pain, which ultimately creates more pain, then to avoid the newly created pain, we engage in the very activity that created the pain in the first place, and so on and so forth. You get the idea. But take note—this circuitous pattern is not limited to drugs or alcohol; we engage in all sorts of behavior and create myriad States that provide a temporary illusion of feeling good, or at the very least, "non-pain." (In truth, it's really not as painful as the perceived alternative and lasts a lot longer.)

If you don't have a conscious knowledge of where you want to go or what your destination is, then you are going to move along blindly, forgetting that all you really wanted is to feel good. What happens if you can't buy things? You don't feel good. You don't enjoy life. In light of what you now know about the effects of State, do you think that a positive State will make it easier for you or make you more effective at creating wealth and getting the things you want? Absolutely. Successful people know it, and now you know it, too.

Strategy

To function properly, brains need neurotransmitters—fuels of well-being—like dopamine, GABA, and serotonin. (For the sake of simplicity, I'm going to refer to all neurotransmitters as fuel.) When your brain creates fuel, you feel good. Drugs and alcohol stimulate the production of fuel by measurable percentages. But this phenomenon is not limited to drugs and alcohol; food also stimulates the increase of neurotransmitters by up to 50 percent (the term "comfort food" may be spot-on!). Sex will increase dopamine by up to 150 percent. Alcohol and THC (marijuana) by up to 300 percent, opiates by up to 750 percent and crack cocaine and methamphetamines by up to 1,200 percent. The delivery of these stimulants to the brain is akin to a supercharger or turbocharger on a car—the problem, of course, is the impossible sustainability of these fuels.

If you try to run this pattern or strategy over time, you will undoubtedly arrive fueled on desperation. You will arrive broken down and in much need of repair. You need a tune-up. This book is going to be your toolshed—the place that houses strategies you can implement to create a happy, fulfilled life. The car is yours—your metaphoric vehicle for your life. This is your shop and you are the mechanic. I will provide the tools and show you how to use them, but you have to do the work yourself. If you don't, you will chug and sputter along the road until the next time you break down...and the next and the next. However, if you play full out, I will show you not only how to do the maintenance to keep you running, I will also show you how to build and modify your supercar to run better than ever.

You don't even have to *want* to do the work, it helps of course if you do, but you have to at least want *something different* in your life. Here's an example: let's say for a moment that you want to improve your health but you don't want to work out. If you work out even when you don't want to, you're going to get results. Your body doesn't care whether you *want* to work out or not, but if you push yourself and do the exercises and challenge yourself, your body is going to respond and inspire you by the results. You can't wait to be healthy, to start doing healthy things. Good health is a by-product of healthy behavior, not the other way around. Five years from now, will you be pushing your rusty old car down the road or taking laps in the winner's circle?

It's important to know that the emotional fuel you are using right now you are generating *right now*. You and I "do" our emotions—we're like power plants. What does a power plant do? Right, it generates energy. And what is emotional fuel? You got it—energy. You and I are power plants that generate energy at will, even subconsciously. As a matter of fact, we literally generate energy *all the time*. A conscious awareness of the way we generate fuel and "do" our emotions will give us easier access to better States, which should allow us to create better strategies for making decisions and taking better actions, thereby enjoying better results. We need to learn new and better strategies for mastering our State.

THE MAP IS NOT THE TERRITORY

Reality and our perception of what's real are never exactly the same; that doesn't make us right or wrong, it's just a perception. You've probably played the game where someone passes through a room or something happens when a group of people are watching. They all saw the same thing, but when you interview them, you get different responses; no two are quite the same. Now they all experienced the same thing, but they each had a different perception. Is any one of them right or wrong? No, it's just their different perceptions and each one is responding to their own experience, not to the reality itself—they're responding to the meaning they've given it.

Now, a map is just a map, right? Well, not exactly. Everyone has a unique "reality map" or model of the world and no one's map is more real or more accurate than anyone else's. It's just different; it's *their* map.

I don't need to tell people when they're doing something that is going to screw them up—they tell me. I just ask questions and make simple statements. We'll talk about their situation with an example of driving off a cliff and I'll tell them that if they keep going like this, they'll probably drive over the edge. Even if I say something like, "You're going off that cliff!" they'll probably say, "Ha! Screw you!" and keep on going. But if I come from a different angle, sit down next to them and ask "where are we going?" they're more likely to talk to me. It's the same principle for effective communication with a child, the best way to talk to them is to meet them where *they* are, not where *you* are. That means stooping down so you can be eye-to-eye. Now, if I respond without judgment, just with understanding, I can help them determine their own outcome and work through the process. The problem that many people have, including therapists, is that they always know best and tell their loved one or patient what they think—they put their own map on someone else's territory—and that someone keeps telling them that it doesn't work, the map just doesn't make sense to them. It's still the same principle: When someone else tells you something it means nothing, but when you tell yourself something, it means *everything*. And even though you come back and tell that person they were right, you'll still make the same mistake until you believe it yourself. Sometimes it just comes down to a matter of choices; you need variety to expand your options and find your own map for the territory.

Story

This is probably the most fun part of your journey. You're in your dream car, you've just filled up with premium fuel, and you're in a good State—you are full of hope and operating from good, resourceful emotions. This is the part where you get to choose where you want to go, the route you will take to get there, and how fast you want to drive. There's an open road in front of you called "your life." This is the perfect place to start transforming your life story, so let's begin with a short... well, *story*.

One day this guy named John died and when he got to the pearly gates, he met St. Peter who welcomed him into heaven. John immediately noticed that heaven is more incredible than you could ever imagine—everything tastes better, everything smells better, the colors are more vivid—in fact there are more visible colors in heaven than on earth because you no longer have limited, human eyes that prevent you from seeing all the real colors. It's unbelievable—absolutely stunning! What's more, you have your own soundtrack and the music is so awesome you're blown away—your favorite music, just a million times better! Naturally, John walks around checking heaven out when St. Peter taps him on the shoulder and tells him that there is one rule he must obey, otherwise he's free to enjoy all of heaven. The rule is that he cannot go through one particular door marked "private." John thinks to himself, Only one rule? Easy! *and comes up with a strategy to avoid the door. As a matter a fact, he considers all the things he can* do to make sure he doesn't go anywhere near the door because he knows he's easily tempted (as most of us are). John knows that when someone tells him not to do something, he wants to do it all the more. While he's checking the place out, he eventually realizes that he's getting closer and closer to that door. One day John finds himself right outside the door and notices that it's slightly ajar, so he opens it a little more and peeks in, then goes all the way. Instantly, his soundtrack goes away, the vivid colors go away, and it gets sort of gray. Then he notices that the room is filled with boxes—big boxes, little boxes, different shaped boxes—and they all have writing on them. As he looks more closely, he realizes that each box has a name written on it with a birth and death date. He also realizes that the names are all people he knows! Now he starts wondering where his box is when, lo and behold, there it is! John stands over the box with his name on it when curiosity gets the best of him—he leans over to open the box and as he does St. Peter shows up out of nowhere and says, "John, God gave you only one rule in heaven, to not go through that door and here you are!" On seeing Peter, John is so embarrassed that he tries to backpedal, but it's too late—he's caught. St. Peter tells him that it's okay, he can open the box, but before he does, he needs to know what is inside, which is every laugh he lost, every smile he missed out on, every joy he could have had, all the love he could have had, every experience that would have brought him the utmost peace, excitement, passion, and adventure—everything he thought he was living for but missed out on because he played small and didn't give his best. And once the box is opened, he will feel the regret of all those experiences that he missed out on. It will be like experiencing hell—meeting the person he could have been but wasn't because he failed to experience all the pain and all the joy that he could have had.

Now, let's say you are John, would you open that box?

One of my goals in this book is to help you experience life to the extent that, when you get to the end of your days, you'll live a life of such joy, such passion, such adventure, such creativity, such incredible excitement that your box will be so damn small that you won't even be interested in looking for it. You would have lived and loved to your highest ability. Isn't that the life you really want?

If it is, you've got to start telling a different story; you've got to stop and change the question. You can't *not* think, you can't stop asking questions, your brain is constantly going, *"What does it mean, what do I have to do? What does it mean, what do I have to do?"* And since nothing has any meaning except the meaning you give it, this could be the beginning or it could be the end.

Stories are how we learn—they are the allegories that represent our lives and we are the protagonist, antagonist, producer, writer, star. We are all the parts, all the experiences, all the emotions in the story we create. What story are you telling? You always have the power to write a better story and to stop listening to other people's bad stories that influence and affect your State.

The question you must ask yourself (the quality of your questions determines the quality of your answers!) is, *Are you writing yourself as a victor or a victim?* Your story involves trauma—it has to. Imagine a book where Chapter One reads, "everything is good," Chapter Two reads, "everything is still good," Chapter Three reads, "see Chapter Two," etc. Without drama you have no story worth telling, you're simply living a life of convenience, running the same patterns day after day. It's like poor quality gas; you chug along in an average State with no passion, no adventure, just a middle of the road life. Until you change your patterns, adopt a more resourceful, happier State, and get out of second gear, you'll go on living a life of convenience, which is never a fulfilling life. You need drama for an exciting story—you need to be dynamic and play all out! Change your strategy and upgrade your State and tell a better story—it's *your* life!

Let's say I come to visit you and walk over to your TV where you are streaming music into the room and change the station. You've just gone from loud, upbeat, energizing music to loud, sedating pan pipes. What would you do? Would you settle for the pan pipes or rebuke me nicely and go back to the happy music? Millions of people would let the pan pipes play and avoid confrontation and tell themselves that they are being considerate and flexible. The problem with that is, it's *your* story! When you let people come in and mess with the story you want to tell, you are giving up control and leaving the outcome to someone else. That's what we do with negative self-talk also—that voice in our head that needs reprogramming. We keep telling ourselves negative things and playing the same music that we don't even like over and over again, yet we have all the power we need to create a new story—to change the music!

It's pretty much impossible to tell a new story when you're busy telling an old, negative story and rehashing bad experiences. That's like living your life from your rearview mirror—how can you write a new story when you're looking back all the time? Instead of looking where you're going, you'll go where you're looking—right back to where you were when everything started going off the rails. Stories carry lots of emotions; they make you feel certain ways—they can either change your State to a positive one or bring you down and keep you running old limiting patterns. You can't be a worrier if you want to be a warrior.

Remember Dorothy and her pals in *The Wizard of Oz*? Dorothy always had the shoes; she could have gone home anytime she wanted. The lion already had courage, the scarecrow already had a brain, and the Tin Man already had a heart; they just kept telling themselves a bad story based on a terrible strategy and a negative state—and we know that any decisions we make from a bad State will not be very resourceful. Dorothy had the power to write a better story from the very first day, but she believed the lies she kept telling herself and others. It's only in the context of the meaning that we give something that actually matters.

Birds of a Feather

Just like the person who challenges himself to greatness in sports or business, when push comes to shove, that person will have more resources available to them when the times comes to take it to the next level. The person who plays the six-year-old is not building his game. If he ever gets in front of a pro, he'll be completely dominated because he has not grown; he has not committed himself to advance his position. When I play golf with better golfers, I play better. That's the way it is with almost everything in life. So, when I have choices to make, I consciously get as present in that environment as I can so that I can get the most out of it. That's what most successful people do—they don't play inferior opponents, they get up and play with the best.

Have you noticed that people who make a lot of money surround themselves with other people who make a lot of money? Energy attracts energy! Even a nonconformist will find groups of other nonconformists to bond (or conform) with. They do! That's because it is a human need. You'll learn shortly the top four reasons for that behavior, but here's the thing: when you're feeling stressed out, bothered, challenged, or any other unproductive emotion and you're in that negative State, what kind of strategy do you think you're going to use?

The one that challenges you or the one that's easy? Of course, the easy one—it's more normal, the one we are most comfortable with—and then we make an excuse for avoiding the challenging one like, "It's too hard!" and we go back to the easy behavior patterns because they are the nearest and dearest, even though they are probably what got us into the negative situation in the first place. They are our go-to coping mechanisms—the ones we need to change in order to get better results. Unfortunately, when you're trying to cope or deal with a challenge, when you have a need, you will sacrifice your values to meet your need. We all do it. When you're in a crappy State and you need to feel comfortable again, even though drugs and alcohol are hurting you, you use the same thing that got you there because it is familiar to you and changes your State. It gets you into a comfort zone for the moment, but you know that it's not sustainable. You need to get more behavioral flexibility in State management and for that you need emotional mastery. Only by implementing a different strategy can you change to a more resourceful State. Keeping the "birds of a feather" concept in mind, you will find that working new and better strategies will be much easier for you when you surround yourself with people who have learned good techniques for managing their State. When all is said and done, you won't be able to find boxes for your friends or yourself because you have surrounded yourself with people who play all out and you've stayed in the game.

Now, what about your story? What kind of story are you writing? Yep, *an epic!* One with heroes and villains, adventures and misadventures, loves and losses, and most of all, a happy ending—a little box with nothing in it (well, maybe a few Academy Awards for best picture, best actor, best director, best producer...and most of all, *best screenwriter!*).

Here are a couple of ideas to help you write your story:

- Surround yourself with people who believe in you to create higher accountability.
- Hang out with people who are living the life you aspire to have.
- If you are unhappy you will tell an unhappy story—change your focus and tell a better story!

Leverage

One of the ways to get lasting change and the transformation that you need in order to write a new story is through leverage. Leverage is what gives you power over something else; it's an advantage. Imagine there is a giant boulder in front of you and you walk up to it and try to push it over. Would you be able to do it? No. But if you took a little rock, put it right in front of the boulder to use as a fulcrum, then took a long stick and put the short end under the rock, you would have leverage. And the bigger that stick is, the more leverage you would have and the easier it would be to move. But if you took a little tiny stick and try to do it, would you be effective? No. The stick would break and then you'd say that leverage doesn't work. However, if you thought about it and realized that what you need is more leverage and got a bigger stick, what would happen? The bigger the stick, the easier it would be to move the rock, right? Think about emotional leverage then—what is it? In this context, it is what drives you—it is passion, courage, awareness of your emotions. When you come right down to it, the emotional leverage we are talking about—the boulder—is *pain*. (Between pleasure and pain, we are wired 10 to 1 for pain—that means we are 10 times more sensitive to pain than to pleasure!) Leverage for us, then, is non-pain, which means our goal is to get leverage on our pain so we are in a non-pain situation. Consider this: Why are you reading this book? Could it be that it was too painful *not* to read it? In other words, you knew there would be potential solutions in this book to help you overcome painful or negative situations, so to not read it would be like giving up an opportunity to heal, to put yourself in a non-painful situation. How often have you heard someone (or yourself) say, "I am glad I don't have to live like that anymore!"? What they or you were actually saying is that at the time you took your drug of choice (DOC), you were doing it to get out of some kind of pain. We all have a different language for it, some people call it boredom, some people call it feelings, some people call it escape—the presupposition is that if all you did was take it to feel good, you were not feeling good beforehand (you were feeling some level of pain). Now that you know the philosophy behind leverage, you know that reading this book is one of the ways to get leverage; you either bought this book or someone gave it to you as leverage—the big stick that enables you to move boulders and transform pain.

Right now, to get leverage, it is time for you to unleash the demons that have been holding you hostage. You're going to reveal to yourself what the fear of not being enough has cost you. Using a pen and paper, you are going to answer some key questions that will help you accomplish that—you are going to prime your pump. Go as deep as you possibly can so that you can recall as much as you can of that extraordinarily heavy stuff that gets in your way and you can't seem to get past. You may be tempted to minimize, rationalize, and justify some situations (it wasn't *that* bad, I did that because of this or that) but you're not going to do that. In order to be effective, you need to be as honest with yourself as you possibly can. Like a compound bow, the more pressure or resistance you give it, the more forward momentum you are going to get and the farther you will go. That piece of paper is going to be your healing, your forgiveness. You know that thing that you don't want to talk about with your therapist? This is a good time to write it down; you're not going to talk about it with anyone; you are just going to peel back the layers and expose the roadblocks that have kept you from your true destiny.

Here are some of the questions to ask yourself:

- If you were to expire right now, what would be in your box?
- What have you missed out on?
- What has addiction, especially the behaviors behind it, cost you?
- What fueled the addiction?
- Who's no longer in your life because of negative past experiences? Who have you pushed away?
- What experience did you have as a result of living in fear (were you afraid to change, afraid you couldn't change, or that you would never change)?
- If you spent years in addiction, there are a lot of opportunities, a lot of last chances that you missed out on. What are some of your regrets?
- What relationships have changed as a result of bad experiences?
- What are some of your hurts—what is all of this costing you?
- What is the worst thing, the most terrifying thing, that has happened to you?
- What is one thing you won't say out loud?
- What are some of the stories that you tell to shift the blame from yourself?
- Who or what else do you blame?

What you just wrote down is what it has cost you to live in fear—to create your boulder—it's a tough exercise if you do it wholeheartedly. It will leave you in an uncomfortable State at first, but you don't have to stay there. You control your own State. When you've finished answering those questions (or need to take a break), stand up. Loosen your shoulders, shake your arms, roll your head around a few times, and stretch your arms overhead, looking up as you do it. Hold that pose for a few seconds. Alright, how quickly were you able to change your state? Pretty quickly, right? (We're going to talk about that a lot throughout this book because changing your State is the key to shifting almost every negative emotion in your life to a better one—if you're willing, you're going to master priming your pump and filling up on premium fuel, increasing your leverage, every day!)

How many times has a family member told you (or maybe you told someone else) how your behavior was affecting them? How did that feel? Bad, right? The pain finally got bad enough that you decided things must change, you believed that you must change them, and then you picked up this book because you believe it can give you leverage—that's just step one. Now, step two is that you have got to interrupt that old limiting pattern that got you into this situation in the first place. Now these patterns are more than just habits, as a matter of fact, it would probably be fair to say that the word "habit" came up sometime before it became "addiction." But we are clearly running other patterns as well because drugs and alcohol were not the problem initially, they were the solution. So, if the solution (drugs) is the pattern (thought process) that we're running, it must be interrupted in order to run new ones.

Interrupting Old Patterns

Think about the worst movie that you've ever seen, that you would never, ever, want to see again. Would you buy the DVD, get an 80-inch television and top of the line sound bar, and play it all the time? No? Why not? Because it's annoying and makes you feel crappy, right? Yet here you are, running this internal conversation—this bad movie—all the time and fully associating with it. Now, imagine holding that DVD and running a knife across it a few times, then putting it back in the DVD player. What would happen? It wouldn't play! So if all you did today was interrupt one of those old patterns that you've been running, one of those old thought processes, it would be a great day. (By the way, that explains in large part why some people can do okay with only a thirty-day rehab stay—they've interrupted a pattern long enough to be effective. The new pattern or DVD may not be particularly compelling, but it would be better than the garbage that was being played before.)

So, the first step is to get leverage, the second step is to interrupt the old limiting pattern (DVD), and the third step is to replace that pattern with something else of your choosing, otherwise someone else might put a movie on for you that is worse. You have to create a new, compelling pattern and condition it until it becomes a habit—get it into your nervous system—create a new environment. Since you're always running some kind of program, you must decide if you want to be the leader and write your own pattern or if you are going to allow yourself to be programmed by something or someone else. Are you going to be codependent on your environment or independent and choose for yourself? Remember when God had the earth all by himself? Not so hot, right? But when you co-create, you use the resources that are available to you and create a new, compelling story.

The three mantras that you need to be a part of your belief system and applied to your life are: *things must change, I must change,* and *I can change.* And in order for you to have lasting change, you need leverage in order to interrupt old patterns, create new ones, and condition them until they become habits.

PLAYBOOK EXERCISE

Conditions for Your State

For every emotion or State that you want to *experience*, write down the conditions that need to be present in order for you to feel that way. For example:

- To feel safe, you need _____ to be present.
- To feel content, you need _____ to be present.

For every emotion or State that you want to *avoid*, write down the conditions that need to be present to accomplish that. For example:

- To feel angry, you need _____ to be present.
- To feel scared, you need _____ to be present.

Keep your answers handy as you continue reading and working toward fine-tuning your engine.

CHAPTER 2
The Behavioral Trinity

OUR BEHAVIOR PATTERNS

Everything we do is to change our State... our State of being. Anger is a State, frustration is a State, love is a State, depression is a State, and so is humor. Pretty much every emotion we have equals a State. The Behavioral Trinity helps us understand and manage our State using physiology, focus, and language to interrupt old behavior patterns and implement more resourceful strategies. We need to have lots of flexibility and multiple strategies to be successful (and to keep things interesting and dynamic!), and this is where we find them.

Physiology

In the Behavioral Trinity physiology is one of the most influential components. Here's a little exercise to orient you with the concept of physiology: Sit up in your chair, put both feet on the floor, and push your shoulders up. Next, take this book and hold it above your head while you're still reading. Now take a deep, cleansing breath... inhale and exhale slowly. Now moan—loudly. If you laughed at that last bit, keep smiling. If you didn't, smile anyway. Smile wider. Hold that position. Now, get depressed. If you hold your head and shoulders high and you keep a smile on your face, you'll find it very hard to feel depressed. Right now, you're happy—or at least you're feeling awake. Did you consume any drugs or alcohol to achieve that feeling? No, you achieved it just by changing your physiology!

Now, if I asked you to get depressed, would you start to change the way you're holding your body? Let me take a guess—you'd start to slouch. Perhaps you'd even look down at the ground and the smile would be gone from your face. Remember Charlie Brown from the cartoon *Peanuts?* There's a strip where Charlie Brown is standing with his shoulders hunched, looking down at the ground. His friend, Patty, asks what he's doing and Charlie Brown tells her that he's standing in his depressed stance because it makes a huge difference how you position your body when you're depressed. According to Charlie Brown, the worst thing you can do is hold your head up high and your shoulders back because you'll start to feel better, and he warns Patty that good posture takes all the joy out of being depressed.

Let's talk about drugs and alcohol again. Do drugs and alcohol change our physiology? Absolutely. Do they change it by a little or a lot? A lot, right? How quickly do they take effect? Immediately? Drugs and alcohol are effective strategies for changing our physiology. The more flexible you are to change, the more flexible you will be in managing your State. Adjusting your posture, your breathing, and your energy will also adjust your physiology—the foundation of State—and the more you practice it, the better you will become at doing it. Eventually, you will be able to change your State in seconds simply by changing your physiology.

Let's look at some ways that we can change our physiology in the moment to prime our fuel tank and change our State. Like Charlie Brown's observation of a depressed stance, changing the way you sit can make a huge difference in the way you feel, too. What if you got up from your seat? The effect would be more drastic—true or true? What if you dance or do jumping jacks? What if you got on the floor and did push-ups? All are ways to get the right fuel flowing, and if you start out by doing them every morning, you're priming yourself for the day. You're setting yourself up for the ride of your life.

What if you filled up like this several days in a row, and, while you were doing it, you focused on all the good things in your life? What if while you are in this State you focused on gratitude? How would your life feel day after day? I'm not saying you wouldn't encounter the occasional roadblock or detour along the way, but you'd be much better equipped to handle them, wouldn't you?

PLAYBOOK EXERCISE

Physiology

The first rule for mastering our State or emotional fuel is to master the way we use our bodies. It goes to say then, that in order to truly control your State, you must first learn to control and change your physiology.

Make a list of 25 different things you can do to change the way you position or use your body. For example: do jumping jacks, stand if you're seated, or sit if you are standing. Split your list into columns of increasing and decreasing energy (waving your arms in the air vs. running in place) to give you flexibility.

Write these ways to change your physiology in your Playbook. Use them every day to prime your State—begin first thing in the morning and continue throughout the day, whenever you need them.

Focus

The second pillar of the Behavioral Trinity is Focus. Changing your physiology not only affects your State, it will also affect your focus. Try this: Hold your arms stretched out on either side of your body like you are about to give a huge hug, palms up. In the left hand, you're going to put all the good things in your life, all the things that bring you joy, and all the things that you love. In the right hand, you're going to put all the bad things, all the problems, all the things that cause you pain. What shape is the mess you are holding in your right hand? What color is all that bad stuff? What's the texture? What sound does it make? Answer the questions out loud. Now, what's happening with your left hand and all the good stuff? Aha! You have no idea because you were too busy focusing on the bad stuff! You put so much energy on the bad stuff that you gave it color, texture, and sound. Is it possible that while you were focusing on negative qualities that weren't even there, you let all kinds of amazing, beautiful, and happy things slip through the fingers of your left hand?

Here's another way to look at it: When you are angry, what do you focus on in terms of the pictures in your mind? We all make pictures of things that bother us. Do you make them really small, distant, black-and-white, dissociated, out of focus, and framed in? Probably not. You make them big, in-your-face, fully associated, vivid, and in high definition, don't you? And when you are happy, grateful, loving, or in any other high frequency emotional State, do you make those pictures really small, distant, black-and-white, dissociated, out of focus, and framed in? No, of course not. You make them big, in-your-face, fully associated, vivid, and in high definition. See, the things we focus on are the things we feel or experience, and the bigger, brighter, and more associated those images are, the more intensely we feel them. Conversely, the smaller, more distant, and dissociated the images are, the less we actually feel them.

How often do we make pictures in our minds? We do it all the time. You're not alone in this—misery loves company. You are probably quite familiar with this situation: You're at the grocery store where you encounter a friend and you ask how she's doing. Within two seconds she's talking about all the things that are wrong in her life and without realizing what you're doing you start comparing notes or even competing! I refer to this situation as "woundology," and we will dig deeper into this phenomenon—why and how it happens—a little later. For now, just think about it for a minute. How often have you experienced woundology? An old friend tells you something crappy about their day. "Look at my crap," they say. "Look at mine!" you reply with gusto. "Mine is squishy and rough—here, touch it... *smell it!*"

Sometimes we spend precious energy on all the things that are wrong, then when someone new comes along and says, "Look! Look at all the good I have. Look at all the things I'm grateful for!" you and your friend reply, "Easy for you to say. We lost it all. You don't belong with us—go be happy somewhere else!" And the worst part is, that reaction has become not only acceptable, it's often *expected*. We don't celebrate our own successes because it may make someone else feel bad, but we don't hesitate to complain about other people's successes. Why do we do that? Often, it's because the person we are talking to is still focused on everything that's wrong or unfulfilled in their life and we don't want to be a contrarian or be rebuked.

Focus defines how you view your life—it can be like a crappy Instagram filter, a soft camera lens, or flawless and photoshopped. You can either be grateful for what you have or ungrateful for what you don't have. Successful people view bad situations as opportunities to derive something good. They're focus is set on priming their pump and experiencing the best State for the road ahead.

Be forewarned: *boredom is also a State.* Many people fall back into old patterns just to break the monotony, just to feel something other than bored. You can keep boredom at bay by being active and challenging yourself. Remember earlier when we noted that misery loves company? Well, the same is true for success, and successful people surround themselves with other successful people who challenge them to grow and steer them toward a world of engagement. You can do that, too. You can find people who will hold you to a high standard. Hang out with them, learn how they see things from a different perspective, and let them challenge you to grow. If you lie down with dogs, you'll get up with fleas. If you lie down with happy, successful people, you'll get up with—well, you get the picture.

Your Reticular Activator System (RAS)

To help us master focus, there is something in our neurology called the Reticular Activator System or RAS. The function of the RAS is to speed up our ability to focus and make it more efficient. It is a wonderful tool that, like any tool, cares not how you use it—you are probably not even aware that you do use it. Here's how your RAS is experienced: Have you ever purchased something really cool like a spanking new car, a handsome watch, or fashionable handbag—something you thought at the time was totally unique—and before the ink was dry on your signature you saw it everywhere? I have. When I bought my first SUV I thought the color and model was less prevalent than other SUVs. But as soon as I drove it off the lot, the road seemed to be filled with the same vehicle. I thought to myself, *Did they just have a sale? Where were all these cars yesterday?* In reality, were there more of that model SUV on the road than the day before? Of course not—I just activated my RAS's "seek and ye shall find" function. Most of the time we don't even realize that we are seeking because it's happening on a subconscious level and that's where patterns of focus typically work. (Using drugs and alcohol is a very effective strategy for altering the focus of your RAS.)

How many times does a car model get redesigned? If it's popular, it is constantly being improved and fine-tuned, and every year there's a new version of the same model. How many times does a race car get rebuilt? Constantly. In the Daytona 500, a tenth of a second can be the difference between winning and losing. People and sponsors invest extraordinary amounts of time and money to get that tenth of a second—it's that important. You and I are like those cars—little tweaks can be game changers.

If you don't work on mastering your physiology, your performance will suffer. If you don't work on mastering your focus, it will get even worse. You're wired to focus on the negative aspects of your life; discipline is imperative if you want to succeed at focusing on the positive aspects and changing your State at will. You need to commit to waking up every morning and finding something to be grateful for, something that will inspire and empower you. Ever notice how you tend to look for help only when something's really wrong, when you're feeling hopelessly down? Don't put off activating your RAS and consciously focusing on things that will help you improve and succeed. If you are waking up feeling unhappy (or miserable), you might have the added challenge of living in an environment that is full of negativity or toxicity. Readers beware: things and people that bring you the most pain are your personal hells—they prevent you from being happy and fulfilled.

Now you have a number of effective tools to use and proven instructions on how to change your State and your environment, but if you don't actually use them, you're likely to fall back into those easy, negative, destructive old patterns again. All of us, not just those recovering from addiction, are at risk of falling into old patterns. Over the years, those patterns have become all too familiar, ingrained in our thought and response processes. We are prone to run those old patterns when we let down our guard and we go right back to what is familiar—especially when we feel stressed. These are the times when it is critical to activate your EGS and reorient yourself with where you really want to go in life.

Forming Patterns

Now, what we know so far is that all results are an accumulation of patterns: you do certain things, you get certain results. Patterns are habits and blueprints that can form over years or very quickly. Here's a little experiment. Put your hands together and intermingle your fingers. Note whether your left thumb is over your right thumb or your right thumb is over your left thumb. Separate your hands for a few seconds. Now put your hands back together and switch all of your fingers, making sure your thumbs change places, too (if your right thumb was on top before, make sure your left one is on top this time). Feels weird and uncomfortable, doesn't it? That's because you interrupted your usual pattern. Wherever you are right now in life—physically, financially, emotionally, spiritually—is simply a direct result of whatever patterns you've been running. If you want different results, you're going to have to change your patterns. So, while you are reading this book, any time you feel uncomfortable or awkward, then something is probably changing—embrace it!

Your EGS and RAS are closely related. Your EGS keeps you focused, and if your thought patterns are stuck on negative things, then that's what you will feel and experience until you reset your EGS. Say you're driving down the highway and a detour reroutes you to a different, slower road. What do you do? Do you focus on the fact that you're going to be late? What does a GPS do when it encounters a detour or roadblock? It doesn't get upset; it automatically seeks out an alternate route. But you keep asking yourself why this happened to *you* as though it's a personal vendetta when you could be asking yourself how you got so lucky that now you can enjoy the scenic route. Life happens. Bitching and moaning won't move the clock any faster; it will only frustrate you and show in your demeanor. What is most important about a detour is how you react to it—will you allow it to explode into chaos or will you resign yourself to the fact that it is beyond your control and try to enjoy the road less traveled? You always have a choice. Like a GPS, your RAS is very reliable and resourceful when it comes to evaluating alternative routes because it has your end goal in sight at all times. What it cannot do is identify the silver lining in a detour—that is up to you, but if you're all in, you just may realize it isn't a silver lining at all, you're traveling under gilded skies of opportunity.

YOUR BELIEF SYSTEM (BS)

Once you change your pattern, you start changing your life and you get different results. Now, in order to make the changes that you really need to make, the pattern you most have to change is your Belief System (BS). A simple definition of the word "belief" would be "something that you think is true," right? But how do you know? Someone probably told you. How would you define "belief" to a ten-year-old? *A belief is simply a feeling of absolute certainty that you have about a given subject.* Yet, it's just a feeling. Have you ever believed something once and changed? Did that make it not true? All behavior is belief driven: those feelings influence our thoughts, our thoughts influence our decisions, our decisions influence our actions, and then our actions ultimately create our Reality.

There are two kinds of beliefs: limiting beliefs and empowering beliefs. Empowering beliefs help you to feel like you can do whatever it takes, that you can make a difference in other people's lives, that you are sending out ripple effects to change the world. Limiting beliefs just slow you down and prevent you from being resourceful and present.

How many times have you heard someone talk about a kid's parents and say something like, "They must have done some really bad parenting, look at that loser kid!" or, "Wow, they must have been really great parents, their kid goes to Harvard!" As a parent (or just as an adult), think about the results you would like for yourself. What do you really want in life? To be healthy, happy, have peace of mind, more free time, financial freedom, a closer relationship with your spouse or your higher power? Well, in order to achieve those results, you're going to have to take specific and measurable actions—this is where the proverbial rubber hits the road. Now, how much action you take or don't take is determined by how much of your potential or power you tap into, and there are no limits to a human being's power potential—none. You've seen people accomplish things that are nothing short of miraculous, haven't you? The depth of their unlimited God-given potential, power or capabilities they tapped into is determined by their belief patterns. How about you? Have you ever said that you want to be happy and healthy and tap into your higher power, but the reason you can't is because you have no focus, you're dealing with an addiction and just too distracted? Or maybe you're just not motivated and have no discipline. Then your thoughts turn to things like, *What if I fail? What if I succeed? I don't know what's going to happen! Ahh, screw it. I'll think about it later.* That's a pretty limiting belief that prevents you from tapping into your potential.

When we start reinforcing these limiting beliefs with "see I told you—I've got no focus and I'm dealing with my freaking addict son! If he'd just do his job everything would be better. And if I could just get motivated! But I hate discipline so I really can't be successful." It just becomes a self-fulfilling prophecy.

What if you reawakened some of the dormant resources inside you, they started coming to life, and a new belief pattern started to emerge? Maybe you'd start believing that life isn't happening *to* you, it's happening *for* you. Maybe every pain is simply an opportunity for you to recycle that energy into progress. You'd be tapping into an Empowering Belief System that would reinforce that notion that you are indeed out-freakin-standing, you're whatever it takes. Then you could go, "See? I told you so!"

The first thing you have to recognize is that, in order to really have lasting transformation and change, you've got to believe that things must change. How many times have you said that you *should* turn things around, that you *should* take responsibility, that you *should* get your life together? Every time you said "should," what you were really doing was setting yourself up for easily getting out of whatever you were setting yourself up to do—you were creating your excuse. If you said that you *should* go to the gym—are you going to the gym? Probably not and you already know that, you were just *shoulding* on yourself! It's just like people who are active in their addiction, they don't say things like, "I should go get high," they say "I'm going to get high." In order to have lasting transformation you have to believe that things *must* change, or you end up sitting in a stinking pile of "should" instead. You have to take responsibility—you cannot be codependent with your environment—you are the one who must change, and when you can do that, you've taken your power back.

Co-Creating Your Life

Establishing your BS requires a delicate balance—it involves more than just you. Here's an illustration of what it takes to develop balance for a valid BS:

> *One day there was an evangelist going around doing his thing when he comes to a desert. He's walking through the desert when, all of a sudden, he sees an oasis. It's unbelievable! The evangelist thinks it must be a mirage because it's so beautiful until he gets closer and sees that it truly is real—an amazing, beautiful garden! In the distance he sees a house and decides that he must go and tell the groundskeeper how wonderfully God has done! He has to know how much God has blessed him! So, the evangelist walks up and knocks on the door. A man opens the door and immediately the evangelist asks him if he realizes that God has entrusted him with this amazing garden! "Wow!" the groundskeeper says, "I get your passion! Without the Lord's water, soil, and sunshine, I would never have been able to create this beautiful garden! But I've really got to tell you, it wasn't always this beautiful...you should have seen it when God had it all by himself!*

It's all about co-creation! We are co-creating our experiences and our universe. When you tell yourself that you must change, you're the groundskeeper, that's your role in life—God is giving you the tools and the gifts, but you have to take ownership of them. It's not about separation, it's about unification. You have the ability to make choices and the will to make things happen. Your BS must recognize three important things: *things must change, I must change,* and *I can change.*

Where Focus Goes, Energy Flows

People are designed to communicate—we can't *not* communicate. Communication is only 7 percent words (7 percent!), 38 percent is tonality and 55 percent is physiology. Example: someone you know comes into the room looking downward and what's your first question? "What's wrong?" Well, that's not the best question to be asking. What do you think will happen when you ask that question? Either they tell you (oh, boy!) or they say "Nothing." Either way, they are still telling you something. Usually, when they don't tell you, it's because they're too associated to the pain, but maybe you can change their State and interrupt that pattern. I bet you can associate with this scenario: You're pissed off about something and you're having a bad day when your friend asks you what's the matter, but you don't want to talk about it. Before long you're talking about something else and they make you laugh. Now you're feeling much better and when they ask you what was bothering you before, you say, "Oh, it's no big deal, really." And it really wasn't that big of a deal, but when they first asked, you were in a non-resourceful State. When you ask someone who is in that State questions like, "What's going on?" all you're doing is feeding energy into their negative State. But if you can change their focus, then you can approach the situation again and it probably won't matter as much. It's like this: What do you do when a little kid is crying? You change their State physiologically—get them to look up. When they look up long enough what happens? They stop crying, don't they? When your energy is focused down and you're looking down, that's kinesthetic, that's being closely associated to your emotions like the Charlie Brown example. So, if what you're doing is not working, what should you do? Try something else! Successful people know that if one thing's not working, try something else. And if that's not working, try something else. And if that's not working, try something else. They just keep altering their approach until they find the one that works.

Keep at It

Let's say that you have three children under the age of ten and they have all learned to walk. How many times did they give up on themselves when they were trying to walk? Never—they would try something and if they fell down, they tried again until they finally figured it out. Each child would go through different processes until they found one that worked for them—they all succeeded in different ways; they each found their own creative way to solve the problem. One may have pulled herself up by grabbing the dog, one may have hung onto your leg to get started, one may have grabbed the bar of his crib and pulled himself up that way.

Specific Outcomes Require Clarity

Once you have a specific outcome in mind, you need clarity—you need to focus on the purpose yet be flexible on the process. Think of a time when you accomplished something that you were told was difficult, or maybe you told yourself it was going to be difficult. Did it happen the way you thought it was going to happen? Probably not. Now, if you were focused solely on the process, you would never have gotten it done, you'd just be *"Ahh!* This isn't working!" or you'd prove the definition of insanity and keep doing it over and over expecting different results. But when you're really clear on what you want and why you want it, you'll get it done. That's why transformation is such an important part of the recovery process. Just being sober makes you a sober addict—what's the point? What is so compelling that it fires you up to the point that you're willing to do whatever it takes to succeed? You need to have a life that's worth being so sober for that you don't even think about using again. That's living a life of purpose—a life of passion, and that's what we want to accomplish!

PLAYBOOK EXERCISE

Focus

We experience and feel what we focus on: the second pillar of the Behavioral Trinity.

These exercises will help you apply proper focus to different situations in your life. They will teach you to manipulate mental images that bring you pain to make them less painful, and images that bring you happiness to make them even more joyful.

- Make a mental image of a situation that's stressful—nothing too serious, just something that irritates you. Now make that picture bigger, brighter, even closer, and put yourself right in the middle of that picture so you can fully associate with it. Do you feel better or worse? Worse, right? Now take that original image and make it black-and-white, unfocused,

> really small, far away, and put a frame around it. Now how does it feel? Minimizing the image makes the situation feel less stressful.
> - Make a mental image of something that makes you feel good—any experience that brings you joy. Make that picture black-and-white, out of focus, far away, and put a frame around it. Do you feel happier than before? Probably not. Now take that original image and make it bigger, brighter, closer, put yourself in the middle of it, and fully associate with it. Does it feel better or worse? Intensifying the image should make you feel more joyful.

Language

As you focus on becoming a master at priming your emotional fuel, you will face some challenges along the way. One of the biggest obstacles you will need to overcome is one that you create yourself: incongruity. You'll find many instances where a part of you wants to do one thing but another part wants to do something else—it's an almost constant conflict that has nothing to do with addiction—it's human nature. If the wheels on your car are out of alignment, what happens? The tires won't wear evenly and the steering will pull to one side or the other. If your engine's timing is off, what happens? People will run for shelter as your car backfires down the road. The goal you want to set for yourself is the same as it is for your car—you want to align all of the moving parts so that it runs as smoothly as possible, and for you, that means your physiology, your focus, and your language.

Language is the third pillar of the Behavioral Trinity. Whatever State you are in, language—both internal and external—will either contribute to, or detract from, that emotion. When you are upset, what do you do? Do you typically express your anger with words? Your girlfriend might say that the situation is a little irritating while you may curse up a storm. Is there a difference between being frustrated and being full of rage? Big one, right? We use language to describe our situation or emotion by giving it a label so that we can experience it viscerally. When you and I experience negative feelings like anger, we use language that focuses on the problem rather than on the solution, or we come up with countless reasons why we can't implement a solution. However, when we're feeling love, gratitude, or joy, we use language that focuses on positives. Have you ever felt yourself get angrier and your language deteriorates as your voice escalates? The same dynamic is in play in positive situations; you can experience more love and laughter just by changing your language. If you pay attention, you'll recognize that you run patterns with language just like you do with physiology and focus. That's why part of the priming process that you should be doing every day involves an incantation. In this context, *incantations are affirmations with tons of emotional and physiological energy behind them.* They are weightier than affirmations because they are more passionate and visceral. An incantation is more of a *declaration* because it has a resolution, whereas an affirmation is more of an inspirational statement. Designing your incantation is something only you can do because it draws from deep within you, from a place only you know—it's a reflection of who you are and who you want to be. Here are three incantations I declare (with passion and energy!) as part of my daily ritual:

- I now command my unconscious mind to access all my internal resources and give me the strength, the wisdom, and the courage to do whatever it takes to continue my sober journey to be the best me I can be now.
- I am a warrior. I am a champion. I am a leader.
- I am a perfect miracle exactly as I am because all I need is within me now.

If you speak your incantations (language) slumped over (physiology) and you're thinking (focus) it's not going to work for you, will it help to change your negative State? Of course not. But, if you stand tall, say it clearly, focus on good things in your life, and speak the words with passion, you will feel the difference! When all of your parts are aligned *in the moment,* your brain will believe what you are telling it, but when they are out of alignment, your brain will know that that, too, and it will tell you something like, *Who are you kidding? This is straight-up BS!* There's an old saying that I heard over and over when I was growing up that still makes me stop and think: *Whether you tell yourself you can or you tell yourself you can't—you're right.* Be mindful of your language—your brain will believe whatever you tell it!

Your language becomes your reality. Much like asking questions to direct your focus, your internal and external language directs the way you perceive your reality and affects changes in your State. If you're telling yourself that this process is stupid, that it won't work, that you're a piece of crap and your life is worthless, you won't be very effective wielding the tools you need to succeed. You have to believe that you are worth it.

NEGATIVE SELF-TALK

- If you talk to your friends the way you talk to yourself, you'd have no friends left at all.
- Don't expose yourself to negative self-talk—you are always listening!
- If you talk to yourself like you would talk to someone you love, you're likely to fall for it.
- What controls your thoughts controls your life.
- Your body hears everything your mind says—don't let it hear things you don't want it to know.
- A positive life and a negative mind cannot coexist.
- Never say anything about yourself that you don't want to come true.
- Your self-talk will either lift you up or tear you down—speak kindly to yourself!

Neurolinguistic Programing (NLP)

Let's dig into why some people succeed and some don't—how we process information. I'm a master NLP practitioner and trainer. If you're not familiar with it, don't let the term concern you—it's just a label. Neuro refers to the brain, language is, well, you know, and programming is just a system or model, and NLP is how we understand the world through our senses because we're sensual beings.

How many senses do we have? Five or six? We know of five for sure and that sixth one is still in question, it seems that some people have it and some don't. Our five senses are visual (sight), auditory (sound), kinesthetic (touch), olfactory (smell), and gustatory (taste), and that's the way we interpret the world—we process it through the different senses. How do you know you're alive? Because you say so, right? But beyond that, you know that you are alive because you're *communicating*—you would say that you know you are alive because your heart is pumping. The creators of this model, Dr. Richard Bandler and Dr. John Grinder, have rather interesting and diverse backgrounds. Dr Bandler was a computer scientist, so "programming" was his contribution to the label (even though it's not really accurate, programming is the term he used and it stuck). Programming has to do with our habitual responses, the systems or mental patterns that we run on a consistent basis—it's the study of the structure of the human experience. Because everyone's experience is subjective, everything you read, everything you experience, will mean something different to every individual. Well, Drs. Bandler and Grinder looked at successful people and asked, *How could one therapist be unbelievably successful and another fail? How could one person in a meeting get breakthrough results and live a successful life while another person at that same meeting did not?* At the beginning, they modeled two of the most successful therapists—Virginia Satir, a family therapist, and Dr. Milton Erikson, the leading, most successful practitioner of hypnotism at the time, to find out why they were so successful when others weren't. What makes one person overcome an addiction and another person not? (We're going to look into that more ahead.) Drs. Bandler and Grinder then modeled people who had phobias. How did one person with a phobia get over it and another person suffer? How can one person suffer horrific trauma from being raped and never overcome being victimized yet someone else can press on and have an incredibly successful life? Drs. Bandler and Grinder identified certain patterns that are consistent in all of them: In our communications, we're always, always, *always* deleting, distorting, and generalizing information. There's no way you could possibly process all the information coming at you at the same time, right? Right now, you are not consciously aware of your blood pulsing into your left eardrum, but now that I mentioned it you think, *Well maybe I am, a little*.

How We Process Information

Have you ever had a conversation with somebody where you discussed twelve or thirteen things, but they only remembered one? It was the most uncomfortable and negative thing of all but it became the one thing out of all of them that they held over your head in an argument: "You said *this*!" and you're like, "Ah yeah, that was one piece of the conversation but did you get the rest of it? The pieces that are *really* relevant?" Of course not, they deleted it. We're always doing that.

Here's a little test to prove my point: Look around the room and pick out everything that is brown—brown clothes, a brown box on the shelf, a brown planter, and the half-dead plant that's also brown, a brown chair, etc. Now, close your eyes and with your eyes closed, think about everything in the room that's metallic. Okay, open your eyes and look around. Are there more things made of metal than came to mind? Sure there are—you just deleted it. How frequently do you or your loved ones focus on things that are brown instead of things that are shiny? It's just being human, you can't take everything in at the same time, especially when you are focusing on a particular object or issue: *Where focus goes, energy flows*! When you focus on one thing, you're deleting other things. We're always distorting information and making decisions about the meaning of something but it's always a bit (often *a lot*) of a distortion.

The other morning when I came into the office, I said "hi," to my co-worker Mark as I passed his office. He saw me pass by, he heard me say hi, but he didn't respond. Not a nod or a grunt of acknowledgement, nothing. Now, Mark and I have always had a good relationship, we've even played golf on a Saturday morning a few times. I sat down at my desk and thought, *What a jerk—what a completely self-centered jerk!* The thought that at that moment he was really focused on what he was doing never entered my mind; I gave the situation my own meaning—I distorted it. We do that all the time—we make up meanings and distort information by blowing it up into a big deal or making it really small and ignoring its significance. Studies show that women tend to make things much bigger than they are while men tend to do the opposite and downplay them. Does that surprise you? Think about a time when you told someone (or yourself) that you have a huge problem and the guy you were talking to says something like, "Dude what are you talking about? THAT'S what you're pissed off about? It's nothing!" Yet, that's just what we humans do, we make all these stories up and give them meanings based on distorted information.

Another thing we are always, always, *always* doing is generalizing. It's a shortcut, we all take them. Here's an example: Let's say I'm walking up to the front door of my gym. I know that when I turn the knob, the door will open. The following day I go to the same gym but the door has been replaced, it no longer has the knob that you turn, it has a lever. I'm not going to think, *Oh no, what is this? Now I have to reprocess information and try to figure out how to use this thing!* No, it's just a freaking door—you push the lever down and open it. You don't give up because you're stumped, you generalize it as "door." One of the most common ways we generalize is by saying things like, "men are..." or "addicts are..." Is it true? No, it's just a generalization—a shortcut.

A phobia is more often than not a generalization. Also because true phobias occur deep in the limbic system, they can be desperately life-limiting. You get labeled a "germaphobe" if you are constantly cleaning things and carrying a bottle of sanitizer in your pocket, but has a germ ever attacked you? Let me elucidate—you don't have a phobia, you're distorting it into one, you're just obsessive. If you're truly phobic you wouldn't be sitting outside reading this book. A phobic reaction to germs, or even the thought of them, would make you hyperventilate and freak out. Take a dog, for example. Let's say a four-year-old gets bitten by a dog and whenever she sees a dog she's scared to death. She's thinking, *Woah, I've been bitten by one of those and I'm scared!* For her, all dogs equate to fear. It's a phobia, it's in her limbic system. On the other hand, if a dog bit you, you'd probably think, *THAT dog bit me so I'm going to stay away from THAT dog*, and when you encounter other dogs, you may feel a bit nervous and avoid them, but you're not going to lose it. It's not a phobia, it's a generalization and a valuable tool in your toolbox. The problem with generalizations is when we use them improperly, when we label things a certain way that is not constructive and often totally inaccurate. How many unfounded and potentially damaging generalizations are you running in your thought patterns? Probably quite a few, but now that you know what to look for, you can relabel them and give them better, more truthful meanings.

PLAYBOOK EXERCISE

Language

Language, the third and final pillar of the Behavioral Trinity, can be a super-effective transformation tool once you master it. In this exercise, you will work on mastering the words that you use for

> maximum positive results. Practice these ideas whenever you can and as often as you can in order to create a new pattern of thinking.
>
> Take at least five minutes and write down as many positive words or phrases as you can. Change your physiology as much as you need to engage your body. If you can, play some music that makes you feel good and think happy thoughts while you write.
>
> Commit to catching yourself when you use words that fuel negative emotions and States. Write down the negative words you find yourself thinking or saying and replace them with better, more resourceful words. For example: Problem = Opportunity.
>
> During the next few days, write down positive questions to your negative ones that presuppose what is great about you and your ability to be transformed. Keep doing that until it becomes a new pattern of thinking for you.

Questions direct our focus. If you want better answers, ask better questions! There's a saying from the Good Book, "Ask and ye shall receive." When you ask yourself questions like, *Why am I so stupid?* Or, *Why am I so fat?* your brain searches for and finds references to support the presuppositions—*I'm incapable of succeeding, I eat like a pig, I'm depressed*—then it shares the answers and the falsehoods spread. You need to rewire your thinking and repose those questions as positive ones such as, *How can I celebrate all that I know while appreciating there's so much more to learn?* or, *What can I do to be leaner and healthier and love myself as I am?* The presuppositions in those questions are very different from the first ones, aren't they?

Emotional Mastery

Knowing what you know now regarding language, how can you manage your State better? Your playbook exercises are key because you've now learned how to access the Pillars of Transformation: physiology, focus, and language. Knowing how to change and manage these components is the fuel that all successful people have in common. You also have a deeper understanding now of how to create your own emotional super-fuel and how to get what you *really* want—not things, money, or anything money can buy—the emotional State of feeling fulfilled. Now you can prime your pump at the start of your day and go full speed ahead with confidence and enjoy the ride of your life!

There are two fundamental reasons why this conversation is such a game changer. The first is: we were never taught how to consciously choose the appropriate State for what we want to accomplish. Using the car analogy, if you were engaging in a race of utmost importance, wouldn't you fill your tank with the appropriate high-octane fuel? Wouldn't you also tune up the entire car, check the fluids, the timing, and the tires before the race? Still, it wouldn't matter if everything in the car was in perfect condition and it was purring contentedly if it had no gas. Like going on a job interview, the State you are in will drastically influence your responses and performance.

Think about how important State management is to top-performing athletes. No doubt you've noticed in post-game interviews that they credit accessing a variety of resourceful actions and emotions (States) in order to be so effective. That's often referred to as being "in a state of flow," "presence," or "in the zone." All the preparation, the practice, the work that super athletes do guards against cracking under pressure, ensures they maintain a positive, resourceful State and continue to deliver extraordinary results. The same is true for intimate relationships. When you are in a non-resourceful, fearful, angry, resentful, or otherwise negative State, that's the same person who appears at work and at family dinners. On the other hand, when you are present, confident, engaged, and loving, that's the person who appears instead. It's a much more fulfilling experience for everyone, isn't it?

What Does It All Mean?

Nothing in life has any meaning except the meaning you give it. This is a tough concept for some people to grasp but it's extremely important. Let's say you are driving along in your car of life and something happens—that "something" has no meaning until you give it one. Do you think the State you are in influences the meaning you give it? *Abso-freakin-lutely!* It's a game changer! When you are angry and someone does something that irks you, what kind of meaning would you give it? You would probably use something non-resourceful such as, *that person is a jerk, it's always my fault,* or, *it's "the man" keeping me down,* and so forth. How about a friend that you hang with, always busting each other's chops? One day you're in a non-resourceful State of anger and your friend teases you about your haircut—how do you respond? Instead of laughing and playing along as you usually do, you take umbrage and lash out. When you're in a funny, open, or loving State, it's all fun and games, but when you're in a non-resourceful State it's inconvenient and personal. Our brains are constantly focused on what is happening at the moment—our current emotional State. They are always wondering what's going on or what we are missing, then asking what it means. Then, and only then, do we decide how we're going to respond relative to the meaning or answer we've attached to the situation. Like computers, our brains are constantly evaluating and deciphering our internal and external environments and assigning a meaning to it all.

How is it that a person can be surrounded by substance abuse and experience extraordinary childhood trauma yet become abusive and addicted themselves or marry someone who is an alcoholic, drug addict, or physically and verbally abusive? How is it that someone else who has been exposed to the same trauma as a child becomes an amazing, balanced person and, even with a busy work and home life, still makes time to help others overcome their own traumas and addictions? Actually, it happens all the time. By helping other people unpack their life experiences I've learned that the difference between a balanced and unbalanced life comes down to the meaning each person assigned to their experiences. For example, I once read of a study on the life experiences of twins who came from a broken family. Their father was an addict who abused both the twins and their mother. One of the twins was in prison for drug offenses and domestic abuse like his father and the other twin became a doctor who never used drugs. When asked why they chose such different lifestyles, they answered the exact same way, *"With a father like mine, what did you expect?"*

At the end of the day, the "State of your life" equals the collective "States of your life." State influences everything! How important is it to you to consciously react from the appropriate State for tasks and decisions? That's a question you need to answer right away—like, *now*.

HOW TO SYPHON GAS

Remember when we were learning about priming your pump and I said that we would come back to the concept of syphoning gas? Well, we're back.

Let's start by agreeing that gas is liquid energy (actually, *everything* is a form of energy). When you siphon gas, you're really just moving energy from one vessel into another vessel. For those who've never had the pleasure (now is not the time to try), it's done by exerting enough force to get the liquid energy flowing freely from the source vessel into the receiving vessel, like this:

Let's say you want to cut the lawn but your mower is out of gas. You see your car sitting in the driveway all filled up and decide to save yourself a trip to the gas station. So, you get a gas can, cut your garden hose to about a three-foot section, and slide one end into your car's fuel tank. The other end you put in your mouth and suck on until it creates a vacuum and you can taste the gas coming through. Next, you take the end of the hose from your mouth and insert it into the gas can. While it fills, you gag and try to spit out the gas you just tasted. Once you have what you need, you pull the end from your car tank, which breaks the vacuum and stops the flow. It's a simple process that tastes terrible and leaves a strong odor in your nose and a tell-tale ring round your lips.

Now, does the siphon (hose) care whether it is delivering gas, milk, or poison? No, the siphon neither knows nor cares what is flowing through it, where it came from, or where it's going. It's simply a tool that transports energy from one place to another. And here's my point: Your brain is a syphon—you can pump clean, wonderful energy from the universe (the source) right into your life. Can you imagine what your journey could be like when you tap into that amazing emotional fuel and run on it every day? You have the tools—you just need to get going!

CHAPTER 3

The Four Tiers of Human Experience

SUSTAINABILITY

Everything that we do or experience in life can be categorized into one of four tiers ranging from sustainable to unsustainable. Understanding how these experiences are classified and where they fit will help you to understand certain behaviors that, in turn, will help you develop more effective ways of dealing with them. All States and behaviors fit somewhere under this umbrella of human experience.

Tier 1: All Good

The first tier, or class of experience, feels good and *is* good. It's composed of things, actions, or experiences that are also good for you and good for others—for society and the universe at large. The qualities in this tier are highly sustainable, which means you can continue to experience them over and over again—even for life, if you want. Think of some experiences that you not only enjoy and feel good for you, they also are good for you. Some people get a lot of fulfillment and joy out of prayer, meditation, dancing, or reading. These behaviors are not only good for you, for many they also feel good to do.

Tier 2: Pretty Good

Qualities in the second tier don't necessarily *feel* very good but they *are* good. More precisely, they don't feel good *in the moment*, but they are good for you, good for others, and good for the greater picture (the universe). One example of something from this tier is exercise. For some people, exercise doesn't feel good at all, especially when they first begin. However, you know that exercise is good for you physically, emotionally, and mentally. It is also good for those around you because when you look and feel better, you interact with others better, and you can influence people close to you in a more positive way. Exercise is also good for society because it improves the overall health and well-being of the general population.

Successful people have become experts at finding strategies to convert tier two experiences into tier one experiences—something we all should take note of in our own lives. Can you imagine how much more you could accomplish and improve in your life if you did more things that are good for you and enjoyed doing them? What a world of difference it would make! You'd actually look forward to tackling those projects you've been putting off. But how do you do it?

Think about some of the strategies you could use to make exercise enjoyable—to convert it from a tier two into a tier one experience. You could change the type of exercise. Instead of lifting weights you could do yoga or try running. You could hire a personal trainer to teach you new techniques and keep you interested. You could listen to music that motivates you while you're exercising to make it more enjoyable. How about playing a sport with friends, like basketball or tennis? You could even go for long walks after dinner alone or with your partner to supplement your routine and fit some quality time into your busy schedule.

While tier two is also sustainable, it is slightly less sustainable than tier one. The more you enjoy something, the more you look forward to doing it and the more potential it has to transform from a task or project into something that's actually fun and provides quality "you" time.

Tier 3: Kinda Good

Now, the third tier *feels* good but *isn't* good. It is not good for you, for others, or for society. Nothing about it is good in the big picture of life and it also isn't sustainable—it just happens to make you feel good. We all can find examples of this tier. When it comes to food, fast food like McDonalds or Burger King fits in this tier. Any activity that feels good but is not taking you and me further down a path of growth is usually tier three. For example, spending unnecessary time on social media, or watching reality shows (which we know are not real at all), or binge watching a series on Netflix are all tier three activities. They may feel good but rarely, if ever, are they actually good for you.

Tier 4: No Good

Finally, the fourth tier is just what you'd expect—it doesn't feel good, it isn't good for you, and it is the least sustainable of the four tiers. This tier is an odd one as very few people are actually aware of behaviors and activities that will fall into this tier. You see, generally speaking, as soon as we find out a behavior or activity, or State, falls into this and we become consciously aware that it does not feel good, nor is it doing any good for us, our brain will find a healthier alternative. A good example of this is living in a State of depression. Someone who runs this pattern may not realize they have worked themselves into habitually running "depression" and not only does it not feel good, there is no upside. Once the brain becomes conscious of this double emotional bind, it will create a new pattern that will at the very least feel a bit better or "good" in comparison. What was once a tier four experience can then be replaced by a temporary tier three experience and the loop (pattern) starts over.

Shifting Tiers

In what tier do drugs and alcohol belong? Most of the time they start out in tier three—you know they are not good for you but they feel good. You also know that they are not good for the other people in your life nor are they good for society as a whole. Eventually, they don't even feel good but you've come to a place where using them feels better than not. Your only alternative is a "feel-worse" option, which hardly seems like an option at all, until the effects of addiction wear off and being without drugs feels better than taking them. Most people don't even consider stopping or seeking help until tier four has been not only achieved but is experienced for some time—until they have a conscious awareness of themselves and rationalize it: *I only use so I don't feel like absolute crap; I never actually feel good, I'm just not knocking on death's door for a little while.*

What else fits into tier three or four? How about food? Let's take fast food, for example. For most people, fast food is a class three experience—they enjoy it, they know it's not good for their health, and they know it doesn't contribute to a healthy family or society. For other people, fast food is a tier four experience—they avoid eating it because they know it's not good for them and they no longer enjoy eating it.

What about food like salad—like spinach or kale? They can be categorized as a second-tier experience—you don't necessarily enjoy them but you know they're good for you. Now take that spinach or kale and blend it in a smoothie with bananas or strawberries. Did that "salad" just move up to a class one? It definitely did for me. Suddenly, green doesn't taste so...*green*.

States can also be categorized into these tiers. Take anger, for example—it neither feels good nor is it good for you. Or maybe to you it *does* feel good, but it's still not good *for you*. Is it sustainable? Absolutely not—feeling angry will eventually climax and the outcome won't be good. Fear is another example. Perhaps you've felt fearful approaching a tenuous situation and it helped you tap into resources that kept you from getting hurt. It didn't feel good in the moment but ultimately it was good for you, so you'd categorize it as a tier two experience. However, if you constantly live in fear, you will miss out on great opportunities and experiences and your fear will become detrimental—it will neither feel good nor will it be good for you, so you'd categorize it as a tier four experience.

Most class three experiences will naturally turn into class four experiences over the course of time. However, converting a class two experience into a class one experience is an *active choice*—progress is not automatic. This is a very important point to understand about change—it's the equivalent of shifting gears in your car. You know that to go faster you have to shift up—you have to be in the right gear in order to perform at a higher level and to be successful at sustaining that speed. Very often we are trying to start a new journey from fourth gear. If you have ever driven a stick shift, you know that starting from a complete stop or slow roll in fourth gear is near impossible. The car will almost always stall out. It is vital that we are aware of where we are, what gear or tier we are in, and what tier is going to be the most effective for progress. Only then you can enjoy a nice, smooth ride.

CHAPTER 4

The Six Human Needs

A STRATEGY FOR FULFILLMENT

How do you create change? You need a reason, right? Think about the last major change that you made in your life: how many reasons did you have to make that change?

What if I told you that there are six reasons that drive you to change? Actually, these are the only six reasons that we do anything—they drive all our behavior. My mentor and friend, the great motivational guru Tony Robbins, identifies them as our *six human needs*. While everyone is unique and requires them in different proportions and hierarchies, we all need each one of them. More than likely, what you've been calling "reasons" are actually "strategies" to help you satisfy those needs.

All States and behaviors meet the first four needs, called the Needs of the Personality, and fall into one of the tiers. Like food, we must eat to survive in order to meet our need for fuel, and like food, that fuel can be positive, negative, or neutral. Take it from The Rolling Stones, "you can't always get what you want, you get what you need!" So it is in life—we often can't get our wants but we do get our needs. Just ahead you're going to learn about the Four Tiers of Experience (sustainable and non-sustainable conditions) and why we will sacrifice or violate our values in order to meet those needs.

1. Certainty

Our first need is *certainty*, which is a survival or instinctual need. Every State and every behavior will meet this need of predictability and assurance. Certainty is a guarantee that things will happen in a particular way. It is safety, security, comfort, control.

How does uncertainty make you feel? Think about a time when you felt absolutely no certainty—when you had no idea what was going on or what to expect. Does the word "uncomfortable" come to mind? What about "anxious," "nervous," or "vulnerable"? What did you do to regain a semblance of certainty or control? What positive or negative behaviors or States did you engage in? Did you ask questions? Lots and lots of them, I suspect. When you're going somewhere you haven't been before, you're likely to ask questions like: *How do I get there? What should I expect? Who else will be there? What will the weather be like?* And so on. If you're buying a new car, you ask about the model and the performance—you might even look up reviews and videos online so that you learn as much as possible about what you don't know.

Let's say you're going to a seminar to hear someone speak for the first time. You get there and randomly choose a seat. Halfway through, your phone vibrates in your pocket so you walk outside to take the call. When you come back, would you take the seat you just left or would you choose a different one? Odds are, you would choose the same seat or one nearby. Why is that? It's your need for certainty—you don't know what will happen in the next few minutes or hours, but you do know something about that particular seat: you know what view to expect, you know what temperature to expect at that particular spot, you feel safe there. But what if you came back and someone else is sitting in that chair? It's *your* chair, right? You feel "off," maybe a bit upset, even. Do you choose another seat in the same vicinity? More than likely you will.

How do you gain certainty in unknown situations? For one, you're likely to change your focus and instead of homing in on what you *don't* know, you focus on what you *do* know—you may say to yourself things like, *It won't last forever*, or *How bad can it be?* You can also gain certainty through a variety of substances. Have you ever heard of "liquid courage?" Alcohol takes the edge off, it makes being uncertain more comfortable. Or maybe you're inclined to smoke a little weed to ease your anxiety. Whatever your drug of choice is, you know it well—you know it will give you the comfort you're looking for.

How about this: do you think someone could derive certainty from lying? Absolutely—the ability to control the facts or manipulate the situation changes their State.

Now that you're seeing more clearly how your need for certainty influences everything you do, what about your career choice—the job you do? Do you need a fixed salary or fixed hours? Certainty-driven people are more likely to work in an industry that is as recession proof as possible, or join a union and be guaranteed a pension. Certainty-seeking people are apt to choose careers in industries with a constant demand, like health care, plumbing, or civil service. They can pretty much expect a consistent pay rate, work schedule, and demand for services, and that certainty makes them happy or at least comfortable.

How are certainty-driven people in relationships? They ask questions all the time like, "How are you feeling? What are you thinking? Are you doing okay? Are we doing okay?" They may even say things like, "Where were you at four o'clock when I called? You didn't pick up or answer my texts, but I see you've been posting away on Facebook!"

Do you think certainty-driven people are clingy or codependent? Absolutely. They need reassurance, and lots of it—they need to know that they are safe in the relationship. Some certainty-driven people may even behave in a very controlling manner by monitoring social media, checking phone records, and questioning someone's behavior. Undoubtedly, you've noticed myriad strategies that help you satiate the need for certainty; the question now is, what tier of experience will it fall into?

We all seek experiences, behaviors, things, and even people who give us certainty on some level—it makes us feel safe and comfortable, a little less chaotic. You know that place called the "comfort zone"? I call it the "certainty zone" because it's not always comfortable there—*certain* or *familiar* are more accurate descriptions.

2. Uncertainty or Variety

The second of our six needs would appear to be in direct conflict with the first need, it is *uncertainty* or *variety*. We need change—we need to avoid boredom—and variety is the spice of life! While ordering a particular meal at a restaurant will give you certainty, ordering the same meal every day will likely become boring and eventually unappetizing—it's going to lose its appeal.

Uncertainty is an extraordinarily important need—it's where the juice of life lies. It is not only important in essence, it is also important because it's the one need people suffer a deficiency of most often—we simply do not get enough uncertainty or variety in our lives. Why is that? Why are we so hesitant about being uncertain? Because there's risk involved. To some people, that means discomfort and vulnerability. It can even be equated with pain. But you have to risk something in order to gain something. As a matter of fact, success is directly proportional to how much uncertainty you can comfortably live with. The more you risk, the more you can potentially reap. Remember the clichés *no risk, no reward* and *no pain, no gain*? Of course you do—they're ubiquitous because they are true!

People who are comfortable with risk love knowing that so many others are uncomfortable with it and will do almost anything to avoid it. They know that the rewards of uncertainty can be life-changing, and they surround themselves with people who understand and embrace it. Most of the rest of the world are stuck in the realm of hesitation—it's a second-tier experience and they know it can be good, but they just don't enjoy it, so they dip a toe in and hesitate, but they are never all in.

Remember that needs drive all decisions, so what kind of career path might someone choose whose need for uncertainty outweighs their need for certainty? How about an actor or guitar player? Or a salesperson who earns a living on commission only? Or extreme athletes and race-car drivers? Those are definitely not certainty-driven career choices (pun intended)!

If you want to have an extraordinarily passionate, adventuresome, intimate relationship, how much uncertainty or vulnerability must you be willing to live with? You have to be willing to go deep or you'll get the opposite—a shallow relationship that will only be as fun as it is deep. If you want to minimize the risk of getting hurt, this type of relationship may be what you're looking for; it will be more certain, but it will also be less exciting—risk lets you know that you are alive. True leadership is stepping into adversity—into the realm of absolute uncertainty—*with certainty!*

Let's look at some other ways that you can add uncertainty or adventure to your life. Have you ever been parasailing, scuba diving, or done something else out of your ordinary zone? Were you apprehensive at first? Probably, but instead of focusing on the risk, you focused on having a good time and you went through with it. Most people have a wonderful time stepping out of the ordinary and think back on their great adventure from the comfort of their certainty-filled lives with joy. This bit of variety is like a palate-cleanser for a safe life—a shot of renewal that counteracts boredom.

Understand now that I'm not suggesting you jump off an airplane without checking the parachute, and I mean this figuratively and literally. But this is where the paradox lies. Risk-takers and thrill-seekers will go through a series of checks before they jump off an airplane. They check the parachute, the gear, and the airplane, then, from a platform of certainty, dive into the realm of uncertainty. And that's what you're doing metaphorically by reading this book and working on improving yourself. You're doing the emotional, spiritual, and physical work in order to be prepared to take the massive risk that will yield massive results. Are you willing to live life fully and get your rush by trying skydiving or scuba diving instead of by taking drugs? Are you willing to accept uncertainty and to open up your heart to someone in order to love deeply and fully? Are you ready for that truly fulfilling relationship you've been looking for? You can have it if you really want it and you're willing to be smart about it. But you'll never have it if you find someone who is actively addicted and allow yourself to be dragged back down. If you want an exciting relationship you can't pair up with someone who is volatile and emotionally unstable—you may get the excitement you're looking for, but not the variety you want. Do you think someone whose greatest need is certainty is going to make different decisions than someone whose greatest need is uncertainty? Will it be a big difference or a small difference? A huge difference! Check the equipment. Be aware of the risk. Jumping without a parachute is a game changer!

3. Significance

The third human need is *significance*: everyone needs to feel that they are special or admired in some way. As we walk through these human needs, remember that each one of us must meet each one of them in a positive, negative, or neutral way. For instance, why do we choose to excel at our work? Why do we want to be the best at playing point guard, Jeopardy, or Angry Birds? Why do you want to feel like the most important person in the world to your girlfriend or wife? Significance! It's an especially big need for celebrities and politicians who will sacrifice a "normal" life and their own privacy to feel special, unique, important... significant!

Significance also sets us apart from others. For example, there was a time when getting a tattoo made someone unique. Fifty years ago, you didn't see many people with tattoos, but today, "body art" is so commonplace that people who have them get even more of them in order to stand out, inking full sleeves, necks, and faces. You're more unique today if you don't have tattoos!

It's important to understand how your strategy to feel significant affects other aspects of your life. What role do you want to play in the story of your life? Do you want to be a kindergarten teacher, a bikini model, or the president of the United States? If so, you may want to rethink what the image is and where you put that tattoo. This isn't a personal judgement call, it's a societal judgement call—right or wrong though it may be.

Some of us find significance by being the weirdest, coolest, fittest or richest. Wherever it comes from, if significance is your primary need, your life will be drastically different from those who have variety as a primary need. Bodybuilders stick to a strict lifestyle that often consists of eating the same things, taking the same supplements, getting a proscribed amount of sleep, and doing the same exercises over and over again. If you want to be a professional bodybuilder, your desire to be the best will have to be strong enough to embrace such a routine. If the desire for variety is more important to you, the restrictive routine of a bodybuilder will be extremely difficult to master. Your life path reflects your primary needs and the choices you make shape every aspect of it—they can either make you or break you.

4. Love and Connection

Certainty, uncertainty and significance appear to be paradoxically contrary to our deepest need, yet they are often used to meet our deepest need. It may seem counterintuitive, but people will often work their fingers to the bone in order to be special while inadvertently creating an environment where they actually miss out on their deepest need, the fourth need, *love and connection*. We all want love, but many of us will settle for connection, which goes back to how much uncertainty we're willing to live with.

When we connect with someone, we feel close to him or her. When we love someone, we feel yet a deeper connection—a union—with that person. The human need for love and connection varies from person to person; the variable lies solidly in the hierarchy of their needs. Do you think someone whose top need is significance will behave differently than someone whose top need is love and connection? Take for example a class clown—clowns make people laugh, and by doing so, they *connect* with the rest of the class. They get *significance* from making people laugh because the funniest person in the room attracts all the attention. They derive *certainty* from their behavior because they control the activity. *Variety* comes from the jokes themselves. New jokes and antics create new opportunities to make people laugh, which satiates their need for connection, significance, certainty, and, of course, variety or uncertainty—all four needs are met to some degree in this one character. Being a class clown might not be something that you aspire to, but another person might make it their mission because it satisfies so many of their needs.

Another way to meet those four needs is through flamboyance. For instance, I enjoy dressing in a way that is colorful and unique—it fulfills my need for significance because it sets me apart. I also connect with myself (also an important element of connection!) when I choose a shirt in the morning—I think to myself, *Ooh, what am I feeling like today?* A wide selection of textures and colors and accessories satisfies my need for variety, while making a choice and being in control gives me certainty.

Going back to the moment of self-connection that I mentioned above when choosing my outfits—love and connection can at times be totally internal. Some of our States, like melancholy or moody, can come from our need to connect with ourselves. Surely you have experienced a moment when you listened only to old heartbreak songs because you wanted to feel through them? You weren't necessarily going through anything relevant in your life at the time, you just wanted to enjoy the moment.

Earlier I said that what we all really want is love but we will often settle for connection. If your partner has been distracted—busy or distant—and you're not feeling the love, you may choose to connect in any way you can in the moment. Think about it. Have you ever picked an argument just to connect? (Yes, arguing is also a way to connect.) It's not the healthiest or most sustainable way, but it works, and you will meet your need to connect through whatever means possible. You see, love and connection are our deepest needs. Certainty is an instinctual need, so when you're not feeling loved, you become uncertain and do anything to re-satisfy that need—like picking a silly or irrational fight. You don't even know why you're doing it, you just do it. You've heard the phrase, "I only yell at you because I love you," right? The person saying it probably doesn't even understand *why* he said it, he only knows how he *feels*. When you and your spouse are screaming at each other, you're actually connecting. Need satisfied. (At an intense level, mind you, but still.... When one of you can out-scream the other, you become more significant. Need satisfied (more intensely). Further, finding new, random things to argue about will get you variety. Need satisfied. You even feel certainty because you are in control. Need satisfied.

Once you become conscious of what's happening, you can live a more rich and vivid life because you will learn to recognize your behavior patterns so you can change them. By change, I mean *improve* or *regulate* them—you can take the wheel and stop yourself from hydroplaning off the road. Just because you have a 700-horsepower engine doesn't mean that you have to go full throttle; you can make use of that fancy traction control you had installed and drive with caution on a wet road. Train yourself to become an expert driver of your life—know when, where, and how to properly use all the features in your super car.

The mistake we most frequently make is allowing ourselves to become overconfident. Just because you know that your car has certain features doesn't mean that you have to use them all the time; you've got to know when and how to put them to use. I'm giving you tools to better your life, but if you don't use them, you'll be like a clock with hands that don't move—not very effective. Because we are creatures of habit, we keep running the same patterns in spite of new knowledge. Putting them into effect will turn that new knowledge into muscle memory and it will become your new behavior pattern. Break those old habits—replace overconfidence with what you've learned until you make a new, better habit.

So, how do you get the love and connection you truly need? Music, dance, sex, food, drugs...those are all ways to connect with yourself or with others. And who do you get that love and connection from? Yourself, family, friends, and even pets.

THE NEEDS OF THE SPIRIT

5. Growth

Just to recap: your four top needs again are certainty, uncertainty, significance, love and connection. All States and behaviors meet those needs, either positively, negatively, or neutrally. They can be type one through type four, sustainable or unsustainable. You will sacrifice your values to meet those needs because you need them just to survive, but to *thrive* you have to meet two additional needs: growth and contribution beyond the self—these are the needs of the spirit. If you meet the requirements for growth and contribution, you can find fulfillment. True happiness lies in progress and progress is growth—in life, you're either growing or dying. Either way, it's a choice.

Expanding your abilities, knowledge, capacity, or understanding of the world will create growth. Have you ever worked at a job where you knew that you'd gone as far as you would ever go and learned as much as you would ever learn in that position? Did the job become boring? Did you start to become disinterested? As human beings, we have the need to grow and become better people; it's what keeps us alive and looking forward to the next day.

6. Contribution beyond the Self

Eventually, we all need to give back, and that's the sixth need. Maybe you've never been an overly charitable person, but just for a second, think about how you felt in a particular situation when you helped someone else. Maybe it was something as simple as teaching a child how to tie her shoelaces or giving a donation to a hometown charity. Did you feel warm and fuzzy? Did you feel full in that moment? Some people live for that feeling. Once (or while) all of your other needs are being met, you need to contribute to something, to feel like you are part of a greater something, to touch someone else's life in a special way, in order to feel complete. So, how will you live your life? Will you merely survive or will you choose to thrive through service and charity?

Take a special note of this: any State or behavior that meets three or more needs at a high level at the same time and is repeated will become *an addiction*. If it meets more than four needs it will become even more appealing, but all it takes is for a State or behavior to meet three basic needs to create an addiction. Here's an example: Do you know someone who is always depressed? They're depressed so often that they've created an addiction to the State of depression. They are the Eeyores of the world. How certain are these people that they are depressed? Usually, about 100 percent. How much uncertainty or variety do they get by being depressed? Think about Eeyore: If you tell Eeyore that it's sunny out, he might reply, "I'll probably get sunburned." If you tell him that it's cloudy out, he may reply,

"It'll probably rain and I'll get wet." There's always something to be depressed about—a negative way to look at every situation. Variety or uncertainty is 100 percent. How much significance do these people get from their depression? They run around from doctor to doctor until they get diagnosed and prescribed, then they get to be that significant friend—the one who needs special treatment because they're so depressed. Their significance also runs at 100 percent. What about love and connection? They connect with themselves as they wallow in their depression or with others who ask how they feel and offer help. They're connecting at 100 percent, too.

Let's take anger as another example. Do you know someone who's always angry at something? Does he *know* why he's angry or does he simply *feel* angry? On a scale of 1 to 10, how much certainty does he experience being angry? 10? How much uncertainty or how many varieties of things does he have to be angry about? Most likely a 10, right? How much significance does he experience being that angry person all the time? 10? And how connected does this person feel to themselves or to others who try to calm him down? Another 10? When a person runs this behavior pattern over and over, they will quite likely become addicted, and now you're dealing with a "rage-aholic."

With all four survival needs being met at such high levels, people can become addicted to being depressed or angry. But what quality of life do they have? What if instead they changed their State and ran around the room singing? There's only so much running around and signing that a person can do before they break out into a fit of laughter, but that ability to change their State gives them *certainty*. They keep running around and they start feeling new things and now they have *variety*. Then they start connecting with themselves and with people who are watching them and now they have *significance*

AND connection. Before long, they realize that they've made a change for the better and they are now experiencing *progress*—they are *growing* and *addicted* to their new behavior!

Improvement, progress, change—they are all ways to grow. If you decide to change your depression, maybe you will decide to change other aspects of your life, too. Maybe now you have taken control!

Here's the same process relative to drugs: when you take your DOC you get *certainty*. You also get *variety* because you never know what will happen while you're on them. You *connect* when you take them and as you tell others the stories you remember or don't remember. You get *significance* by doing more or better drugs. Now you've become addicted to the drugs and to your four survival needs that are being met. Using drugs and alcohol is an incredibly complex and intense strategy to get your needs met because there is a huge influx of neurotransmitters of well-being crowding your brain when you consume them. It's like hitting the turbocharger button on your State!

Let's take a look at the Twelve-Step Program. It's exactly twelve steps and you know that up front, which gives you massive amounts of certainty. How much uncertainty and variety does a person experience while actively working the Twelve-Step Program? Tons. How much significance do they experience as the share their stories? Tons. How much connection is in the fellowship? Tons! The first eleven steps are designed to help you grow so that in the last step, you can just give it away—all of your needs are met at very high levels. That's why, when it is worked properly, it's so effective.

Make a decision to take control—to find things in your life that meet your needs from tiers one and two. Replace things from tiers three and four with them. By doing that, you will not only improve your life, you will grow and thrive!

PLAYBOOK EXERCISE

The Six Human Needs

The four needs that every State or behavior meets are:

1. Certainty/Security
2. Uncertainty/Variety
3. Significance/Admiration
4. Love/Connection

Our top two needs drive the decisions we make in our life. What are your top two needs?

1. _____
2. _____

If you were to change your top two operational needs, what new needs would best serve you and why?

1. _____
2. _____

As part of your tune up and maintenance plan for transformation, come up with four different strategies to positively and sustainably meet each of the following needs:

Certainty _____
Uncertainty _____
Significance _____
Connection _____

Describe four different strategies that you can implement in order to meet the needs of the Spirit (Growth and Contribution)? Examples: go to a soup kitchen and donate your time, set up an automatic donation to your favorite charity.

1. _____
2. _____
3. _____
4. _____

To make better choices, ask yourself these powerful questions:

- How can I serve even more in quality and quantity?
- What can I learn from this?
- How can I meet my needs and add value at the same time?
- How can I serve at even deeper and higher levels?

Aim for Fulfillment

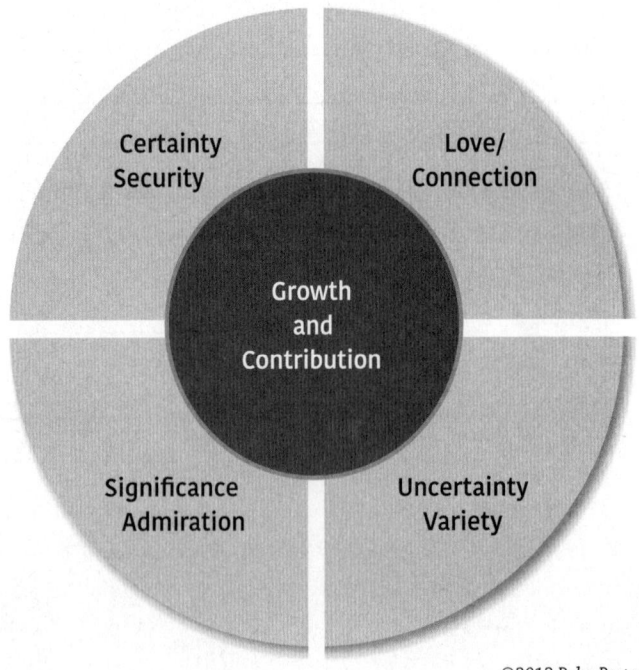

- Certainty / Security
- Love/ Connection
- Significance / Admiration
- Uncertainty / Variety
- Growth and Contribution

©2012 Palm Partners, Inc.

CHAPTER 5
Gassing Up for the Trip

HOW ARE YOU WHY'RD?

How you get there matters—be willing to take the detour!

I have had the tremendous good fortune of being witness to some amazing success stories. In some respects, that's hardly unique—I assert that we all have been witness to some form of success. With unlimited access to information today it would be hard to miss a great story, especially if you are looking for it.

I have noticed that successful people share a common trait: they have a compelling reason to do what they do or to be who they are. Here's an example of the power of this phenomenon: imagine you are climbing a mountain with a friend and you arrive at a steep ledge that you need to get up and over. The ledge is above your head and you do not have much ground on which to stand. How will you get your friend over that ledge? Would it be easier to try to lift him over your head? What if your friend is bigger and heavier than you? Would it be easier to climb the ledge yourself first, then grab him from above and pull him toward you? Well, my hallucination is that pulling him up is going to be easier and more effective. To stand on a precipice without good footing and try to lift or push a large person over your head seems like a losing proposition to me. That approach is much like taking on a project or shooting for a particular outcome without a compelling reason—it lacks a critical "why." I'm not trying to explain how to find your "why," I just want you to understand the *power* of the "why."

As a Peak Performance Lifestylist, my goal is to work with people to clarify their "why" and go deep into that understanding so that they can capitalize on it. Sure, some people seem to be born with dumb luck and a silver spoon in their mouth, succeeding without ever seeming to put much thought or energy into anything, but that's not our reality. In order for you and me to achieve continued success, we have to have a "why."

As it happens, one of my skill sets is the ability to show people how to "WhyR" (wire) themselves in such a way that they are excited to wake up each day and take new steps toward achieving their goals. And that's what we are doing together now—learning how to discover your "why" so that you will look with excitement on each new day and go the distance to achieve your heart's desires. Knowing your "why" will get you there—and beyond.

On a personal note, one of my biggest and deepest "Whys" is my wife Heidi and daughter Ellovie. I am more than committed to provide a life of love, freedom, security, adventure, growth, fun and opportunity. The filter I am constantly running is, *will this take us closer or further from that life?* I also have a strong spiritual undercurrent supporting my "why." As a servant leader, I'm consistently evaluating whether a certain behavior, State, decision, or activity will bring me closer to my spiritual and highest calling. When we tie our choices to our deepest whys or aspirations, we gain incredible power and momentum and the universe or God opens up even more opportunities.

PLAYBOOK EXERCISE

The Power of Having a Why

For an amazing experience, play this exercise full out and full strength. The gifts you will receive and the lessons you will learn about having a clear "why" are more valuable than you can imagine!

1. Stand with your feet together and take your right hand and point it forward. Next, keeping your feet flat and your arm straight, twist to your left as far as you comfortably can go and see where you are pointing. Mark that spot in your mind. Then twist back to where you started and drop your arm.
2. Now close your eyes and visualize yourself twisting as you did before, only farther. In your mind's eye, twist completely in half easily and effortlessly. See that image of yourself clearly. Then see yourself twisting back to where you started and see yourself dropping your arm back to your side.
3. Once again, visualize yourself twisting with your arm extended. Clearly envision your arm pointing, your body twisting, so far and easily that your right arm is pointing more forward than if you would have just raised your right arm and pointed to the side. See and feel and even hear yourself twist that far—almost 360 degrees—gracefully. Now see, feel, and hear yourself twisting back to where you started.
4. Try the visualization thing one last time and make it crazy. See yourself, feel yourself, hear the sounds of your shirt, as you twist like a cartoon character all the way till you

> fully lap yourself and spin like a corkscrew. Now see, hear, and feel yourself coming back in your mind's eye to your starting point, your arm back at your side.
> 5. Now it's time to actually raise your right arm and twist to your left as far as you comfortably and effortlessly can and notice how far you went.
>
> How far did you go the second time? A good 20 to 30 percent farther than you did the first time? Depending on how vivid your visualization is—your "why"—you may have gone even farther!

Mind Power

There are many valuable lessons in that exercise, some we talked about previously and some we'll talk about further along on our journey. For now, let's say that the distance you were able to twist *in your mind* represents your reason—your "why." The distance you were able to actually twist is your outcome. The more vivid your visualization is and the more you continue to focus on it and be motivated by it, the more compelling your "why" is, and that's what keeps you excited and inspired. What's more, it will motivate and inspire people around you to support your goals and dreams. Without that "why" as a motivator, you are on a bicycle without a chain—you can peddle for hours and not move an inch. Your reason—your *why*—is the fuel that will get you to your destination.

Here's an example from my own personal experience of the power of having a "why" and how it enabled me to set a course and reshape my life journey. You may remember that my first career was in the music field. I spent over fifteen years working on some really great projects, contributing in some way or another to the sale of over 100 million records. In those fifteen years, I performed on stage as a musician and off-stage as a producer and an engineer.

For a variety of reasons, the music industry went through a tremendous paradigm shift in the 1990s. (I could write an entire book about the changes, but for now, let me tell you simply that the industry as a whole has been completely transformed during the last twenty years and it will continue to do so in the years ahead.) During the shift, I watched many people succeed and even more people fail. As a deeply compassionate man, witnessing firsthand the pain so many people suffered in that highly competitive environment—as well as experiencing my own personal challenges—caused me to reevaluate my philosophy on life.

But being compassionate has its ups and downs. For one, it allows me to connect with people in very personal, meaningful ways, and for another, it enables me to viscerally experience other people's journeys as they experienced them. But empathy carries its own burdens and oftentimes triumphs and joys caved in from the stress and strain of commercial and artistic failure. My emotions were a roller coaster of dips and curves and climbs of my own experiences as well as those of friends and colleagues. Compassion has always been one of my strongest personality traits and complaining is one of my weakest. So, instead of inventorying my complaints, when emotional conflicts started to eat away at me during those music days, I began to reexamine my life and ask myself fundamental questions, like: *why do I do what I do? What reward do I get from music? When do I feel the most fulfilled? What is my purpose for spending so many years in such a crazy industry? What needs am I meeting?* In order to answer these questions, I had to break down the various roles I was playing and explore my reason for being—I had to determine how I was "Why'rd."

Asking Questions

Maybe you haven't noticed, but as human beings, all we seem to do is ask questions, so I propose that we ask better questions. The quality of our life is determined by the quality of our questions—if you ask crappy questions you will get crappy answers. As computer programmers say, "garbage in, garbage out." Asking poor or shallow questions will render inconsequential answers that won't address core issues where we need to effect change.

Now, I'm not suggesting that simply asking quality questions will create a quality life. However, asking quality questions will provide access to tools that will help you create a quality life—provided you answer them honestly. You must also ask proactive, positive questions. For example: *what am I most grateful for? What makes me feel so grateful for it? What am I most excited about? What about it makes me feel so excited? Whom do I love? Who loves me? What can I do today to share my gifts and my love with others and enjoy the process?* Answering those types of questions will peel back surface issues and get to the heart of our experiences and needs.

The Gift of the Detour

Another key to understanding ourselves is to learn the benefits of adversity, or as we discussed earlier, *the gift of the detour*. When faced with an obstacle, it is critical that we recognize the potential good that can come of the situation. You might ask yourself questions such as: *What aspects of this situation are good? What can I learn from it? What's amusing about it?* When asking these questions, it's important that you honestly and truly answer them, and make the answers part of your being. Asking and answering questions like these is more than an intellectual exercise, you should actually *feel* your answers. Here's a little trick to help you when you're having difficulty coming up with answers: rephrase the question by beginning with "if I *did* know…?" For example, *if I did know what was great about this detour, what could I learn from it?* How to better manage the stress of delays? The unexpected joy of an extra half-hour with an audio book? How a different frame of mind can help me reevaluate a fight with my teenager? *If I did know what benefits are hidden in this manual transmission car that I rented, what would be funny about the situation?* Someone observing me drive like a ten-year-old? Trying to remember what a clutch is for? Figuring out what to do with six gears instead of four, like simpler days? Laughter is good for the soul—you can find humor in just about any situation if you try, and a lighter frame of mind can ignite all kinds of good ideas and positive emotions.

Driven to (a Good) Distraction

Being an artist and performer produced great rewards for me (my "why"). I had many wonderful opportunities to connect with people of all backgrounds, ages, and musical interests. Often, I was in the perfect position to step up and become a distraction for other musicians as they went through the insane rat race of the music world. I would encourage them and help them navigate the nuances and protocol of an industry that was new or intimidating to them. And best of all, being a positive distraction and providing a great time to other musicians made me feel great, too, because I got to live the experiences with them, in real time, as their journeys (and mine) unfolded. I was contributing, helping people live fuller lives. On top of that, I often enjoyed a special bonus while, as I created my own music, people would tell me how I helped them get through challenging times. I felt honored to know that my life and my music were beneficial to someone else—and all I was doing was just being myself. That "space" or "distraction" that I provided for them was a very important distinction for me because it allowed others to step out of their daily grind and into a highly creative atmosphere. Today, I still enjoy connecting with new people—I am "Why'rd" for that purpose.

Just by participating in making music as a producer and engineer, I was able to fulfill the "distraction purpose." Of course, it was more than just a distraction, I would coach them into accessing all the magic and miraculous music within. When records that I worked on would sell in the multiple millions, I knew that I played a key role in the lives of all the people who created them—I had a part in making their days better. Even more, I was, and would continue to be, in some way connected to everyone who would listen to that music for ever. I still feel that great sensation today when I hear songs or see videos that I played a part in creating.

As a producer, mixer, or engineer in the studio, my role is to understand what the artist wants and do my best to make that happen. It is truly gratifying to be a part of that process. Artists have a vision for the sound, energy, or emotion that they want listeners to experience from their music. My job is to create the precise environment for their vision to become clear and resonate with listeners. That can mean accomplishing just the right sound and choosing the perfect instrument or arrangement. Sometimes it means many hours of complex coaching in order for the musician to ultimately achieve an outstanding performance. Once a project is complete and hours and hours of work are behind me, one of the most thrilling outcomes is when the musician or band listens to the finished recording and says that it is better than they ever imagined! It's an ecstatic feeling of accomplishment that's beyond words because I am "Why'rd" to create space for transformation and the manifestation of new energy!

The Sound of Service

What I came to understand about myself and the rewarding work I was involved in was profound, and it provided access to more resources within me that I wasn't even aware I had. Remember this: change is automatic but progress is not—progress is a conscious choice, *a decision*. Think of it this way: you are driving down the road of life heading west when a detour sign appears. You take the new path and now you are heading south. Your direction has changed, but are you still headed toward your destination? Are you progressing toward your desired outcome? All actions may lead to change, but not all change is progress. By evaluating my life relative to my field of work, I found that I needed to control my focus in order to progress toward my destination and achieve my desired outcomes, which are to:

- Provide a *distraction* for people that would give them a chance to get out of their own way and enjoy life.
- Provide and create a space for developing and achieving a *vision*.
- *Connect* with people face-to-face and through any means possible.

- Travel and *serve* people from different walks of life.
- Have a lasting impact on others that *improves* their lives.

Now for me, attaining those goals included some huge distinctions. I finally understood when some of my needs and whys were being met. As things became clear, my next questions were, *Is there more to this experience? What would make it even more exciting and compelling?* As I pondered my responses, I realized that creating a distraction wasn't good enough for me. I love entertaining and being a part of that process. I was, however, even more excited when I thought about what could happen if, while creating a distraction for someone, I could also help them learn so that when they went back to their busy life, they could enjoy it more. Or better yet, what if I could play a role in their discovery that would take them back to the rat race with a whole new perspective and they could start living in the *cause* of life, not in its effects.

These ideas got me so excited that I started exploring more opportunities. One of the things that came crashing to mind was the prospect of becoming a motivational, inspirational, aspirational, and transformational speaker. I could use music to entertain people and put on a show while simultaneously providing tools that they could use to live better lives—something deep and compelling for them to take away. I could travel to different places just like I did when I toured with bands. I could connect and learn from new people around the world. Would I have to give up performing and producing music? Not at all! I will always use the power of music to create distractions and provide learning and conditioning. And I would continue to create amazing experiences through music that would align with my desired outcomes. That clarity of purpose enabled me to create an opportunity to work with one of the world's top motivators and life coaches, Tony Robbins. For four years I was on his team as a speaker and trainer and today I am a Senior Peak Performance Strategist that I am today. To be sure, I experienced many roadblocks, detours, and traffic jams on the road to getting that great Tony Robbins gig and I faced even more as I worked to excel in it.

Discovering the Symphony of I Am

Another opportunity that came to mind was coaching. We all have goals that we want to accomplish, yet often we have no idea how to achieve them. Think of life as a football game for a minute; you don't want to do practice drills all day, you want to get on the field and play, yet you realize that being coached is necessary if you are to play on a team that excels. In professional athletics, every sport has a coach. And whether you want to play golf or tennis or a team sport, there are inevitably a variety of coaches offering to give objective guidance and provide their expertise to help you advance. As a music producer, my style is that of a coach. Most of my experiences have been with bands as a producer; my role was to understand the goals of other musicians and help them achieve those goals. I worked on both the big picture and on minor details so the artists could be free to concentrate on the steps they needed to take in order be the best they could be. One of my roles was to create a space that allowed the music to flow in creative ways, leading to—and fulfilling—the artists' ultimate vision. Today I do that, not just for bands but for people as well. Think about it, coaches are like mechanics, aren't they? They have to understand the system—all the parts and all the players—in order to create a smooth-running machine. In my case, my purpose expanded from supporting people's dream to create beautiful music to supporting people's dream to create beautiful music of their lives—their Epic Masterpiece, their *Symphony of I Am*.

Achieving success in anything is directly proportional to the clarity of your "why" (how you are "Why'rd"), which in turn gives you access to the tools you need to create clarity of your vision. We all have a purpose for doing things and once we know what that purpose is, we can figure out the "how" of achieving it. Once we discover the compelling "why," the answer to the "how" will reveal itself in due course. The universe (God) is funny that way—it fulfills clear requests. You've heard the quote "ask and ye shall receive," well, that's just how it works.

Why'rd to Serve

As kindred spirits, I bet that you also highly value having a huge impact on others. When I asked myself why I enjoyed working on big records, I realized that my aspirations included impacting people in both depth and breadth, and knowing that I worked on projects that sold tens of millions of records was incredibly fulfilling. So many souls are touched, distracted in a positive way, and brought joy through those records, which enabled me to touch them all in my own way. Performing in a band on large stages for thousands of people was an incredible feeling, but it can't compare with the amazing sensation of serving people in large groups and sharing tools for transformation. The depth of fulfillment in serving twenty families during a weekend of healing or serving couples with my wife, Heidi, at a relationship restoration retreat, is a blessing beyond measure.

I love to share these personal experiences because they reveal how, by examining your surroundings and the choices you make, you can create the life you desire also. *I absolutely hold that it is possible to live a joyful and fulfilled life doing what you love.* I found that knowing how I am "Why'rd" provides tremendous power that enables me to uncover opportunities that I couldn't see before. It is a consistent thread of energy that is present among successful people—people who are living a life without regrets—a life that is free, joyful, and fulfilled, that adds value to the lives of others.

POWER WORDS

The section below is powerful! Digesting it will help you with your Why'Ring, and will also help you shift into better States, upgrade your strategies, and enhance your story! Service is such an integral part of rewiring and restructuring your life because a self-centered life can never be truly fulfilling. Understanding these words and adopting the characteristics will give you much deeper and much more satisfying relationships. These are words of the heart—make them a part of your everyday language and give them your own unique meanings and expressions in the story of your life.

Step Up!

On the following page is a quick reference "cheat sheet" to the qualities and characteristics of living a compassionate, resourceful life, based on the Twelve-Step principles of AA. Pin them to your startup menu, read them daily, and commit them to heart—they are the words and traits of a fulfilled life.

1. **Honesty**
   - The quality of being honest; adherence to facts; being upright and fair.
   - Truthfulness, sincerity, frankness.
   - Free from deceit or fraud.

2. **Hope**
   - The feeling that what you want can be achieved; that events will turn out for the best.
   - A person or thing in which expectations are centered (the medicine was her last hope).

3. **Faith**
   - Confidence or trust in a person or thing.
   - Belief that is not based on proof.
   - A feeling of certainty in God or the doctrines of a belief system, code of ethics, or standards of merit.

4. **Courage**
   - The quality of mind or spirit that enables a person to face difficulty without fear.
   - Bravery, valor; daring.

5. **Integrity**
   - Adherence to moral and ethical principles; soundness of moral character; honesty.
   - The state of being whole, entire, or undiminished.

6. **Willingness**
   - Disposed to or consenting; inclined to believe or go along with something.
   - Cheerfully consenting or ready.

7. **Humility**
   - The quality or condition of being humble.
   - Having a modest opinion or estimate of one's own importance.

8. **Brotherly Love**
   - A kind and lenient attitude toward people.
   - Generous and compassionate in spirit.

9. **Discipline**
   - Training to act in accordance with certain rules or structures.
   - An activity, exercise, or regimen that develops or improves a skill.
   - The rigor or training effect of experience or adversity.
   - Behavior in accord with rules of conduct; order maintained by training and control.

10. **Perseverance**
    - Steady persistence in a course of action, especially in spite of difficulties, obstacles, or discouragement.
    - In Christian theology, continuance in a state of grace to the end, leading to eternal salvation.

11. **God Awareness**
    - Being cognizant of and accepting the concept of God or Higher Power.
    - Being conscious of a divinity or spirit greater than oneself.

12. **Service**
    - An act of helpful activity; to supply an amenity to someone.
    - A selfless undertaking that provides aid or benefit to others.

Power Quotes

A life of action and mistakes is far better than a life of regrets. You've just enhanced your language with twelve key words and concepts. Add these two quotes to your repertoire; they will give you important things to think about and strength to understand. Like the twelve words you just committed to applying, these words have been very powerful for me.

1. If you are willing to do only what's easy, life will be hard, but if you are willing to do what's hard, life will be easy.

When I broke through some of my fears regarding networking and meeting people, a whole new world opened up for me. Today, meeting and connecting with new people are some of my greatest joys. I have made powerful and steadfast friends by being willing to stretch myself and do something that took me out of my comfort zone. If you are like I was and find it difficult to meet and connect with new people, here's a helpful perspective: you can choose to take an easy path by just living day-by-day, not growing or challenging yourself or contributing in any meaningful way to society. But if you spend your life doing only what's convenient and comfortable, you will be doing so for your entire life and you will wind up dead or dead broke. Conversely, if you work really hard at developing yourself and your work, you can create an extraordinary life that comes naturally. Unfortunately, the truth is that the chains of habit are too light to be felt until they are too heavy to be broken! Take a close look at yourself and the areas where you may be taking the easy path; ask yourself why you are taking that path and where it is leading you. Be truthful—it may be difficult, but it is imperative if you want to live a great life.

2. You don't have to get it right, you just need get it going.

Action is always better than no action—it will quickly move you away from the "paralysis of analysis." We know from simple laws of physics that things in motion stay in motion, while things at rest stay at rest. Be careful that you do not act without thought—use your sensory acuity. Take notice of what is working and what isn't working and adjust your actions accordingly. Like that detour on the road, notice if you're still heading in the right direction and if your actions are taking you to your desired outcome. This is a paramount point in regard to strategy. It's a lot easier to adjust to a situation if you are intentionally dealing with it than if you get blindsided or kicked in the ass. It wasn't all that long ago that cars came without power steering and when your car was in park or not running, it required a MASSIVE effort to turn the steering wheel. However, if you were moving, turning the wheel was a breeze. Try it when you get back in your car—with the engine off, put it in neutral and try to turn the wheel. Now turn the engine on and try to turn the wheel. Just a little easier, right? Like going from impossible to a cake walk! Those are the same dynamic as life situations—they are much easier to deal with when you are in motion. Momentum will move you ahead much more effectively when you learn to anticipate and confront situations as they happen.

Simply by reading this book, you are farther along on your path to success than you know. Studies have shown that just 80 percent of books that are purchased are ever read past the introduction. People don't finish what they start and they fail to realize that the success they seek is tantalizingly close. Did you know that at least 80 percent of success is just showing up? The remainder comes from sticking with it. To quote a great friend, "Finishing a marathon is easy, anyone can do it. Finishing at your best? Now *that's* a champion! Very few do that."

When You Are Clear on Your "Why"

Here's one of my favorite true stories that exemplifies what can happen when you ask better questions and discover your "why."

When I was growing up, I had a friend (let's call him Steve) who lived with his grandparents (I don't remember what happened to his parents) and for many years we were very close. He and I partied together quite a bit during our teen years—somewhere in the 80's. He was definitely up there on the crazy scale. He would do things that were not only dangerous, they were also very likely illegal. He was one of those kids that we thought would end up in prison or dead before he reached twenty. When I was about sixteen, his grandparents kicked him out of the house and he ended up at our house. My mother, with her heart of gold, was always taking in people with challenges (usually friends of hers), but this time it was Steve. I don't recall specifically what he did, but after a month or so my mother asked him to leave. For years it seemed he bounced from house to house or couch to couch staying in the general vicinity of our neighborhood. One day, one of our friends moved to Colorado, and Steve went with him. I later heard he kicked him out, too, and Steve was living in a tent somewhere on his property. That was the last word I'd heard about Steve for several years. Then, in the late '90s, I saw him on the news talking about some type of rock, and then that was it. Nothing more. On my last cycle with the Tony Robbins organization, Steve and I connected on Facebook and then planned a phone call. It was great to reconnect with Steve because what I learned was incredible and great example of the philosophies that I teach.

It had been probably twenty years since Steve and I last spoke, so of course I wanted to know how he was doing and what he was up to. He asked me what the last I had heard about him was and I told him that I'd heard he was living in a tent in a friend's backyard in Colorado. He said that was true. I also said I thought I saw him on the news—something to do with turquoise. He said that was partly true, but it wasn't turquoise. He began to share how his life had become so miserable that he indeed was living in the backyard of a great friend who wouldn't completely abandon him. We had come from an upper middle-class environment so this was a far cry from his original lifestyle. He said that his life was all about sex, drugs and rock n' roll and he had gotten tired of it. Steve was actually one of the most brilliant guys I knew, and if I recall correctly, his IQ test in high school put him in a genius status. This I know because we both got kicked out of high school together and were sent to another school for highly intelligent but behaviorally challenged teens—but that's a story for another time. Anyway, Steve told me about how he had heard about "inner child" work and decided that he was sick and tired of being sick and tired so he decided to make a change and pursue a life of happiness. Drugs were not doing it for him anymore and he just could not believe what his life had become. He openly admitted that he didn't know if the path he had taken was what the inner child journey was all about but he wanted to find out what it meant. He then shared such elegance in questioning that I still use it as an example to this day. It was a very simple query that changed his life forever: "When was the last time I felt happy?" As he thought about it, he recalled that it was when he was collecting rocks with his grandfather. So, he said, "I thought maybe instead of doing heroin, I could go out and collect some rocks." (Of course, he also said that it wasn't easy to just not do heroin and collect rocks instead, but that is essentially what he did.) He would lose himself in the adventure of the outdoors and get more and more present to himself and what he truly wanted in life. The more he did that, the more rocks he collected, and one day a friend of his said, "Those rocks are worth something; you could sell them." Steve began selling them and started earning more money selling the rocks he found than he was making as a server in a restaurant. He was hooked, so he started to invest in his adventures and bought some prospecting gear. He said he had found his passion and prospecting brought him more joy and peace than he had ever experienced using drugs. Now, the story that I saw on the news was not about turquoise, it was about his discovery of the largest strain of aquamarine ever found in North America. It was worth 1.2 million dollars!

Aquamarine is the state gemstone of Colorado, and Steve became a big donator to the Colorado Museum because he wanted everyone to enjoy it. "My friends said I was crazy to donate them, that this was a once in a lifetime opportunity, but I disagreed. I believed that this was just the tip of the iceberg because I found my life's passion and purpose in prospecting. And then—this is crazy—it's as if I manifested it because I went back to a mountain that thousands of people have been prospecting for hundreds of years and discovered the largest strain of smoky quartz every found in the United States by twenty times! And do you know what is found under smoky quartz? Aquamarine!"

I was blown away. Not only was I so happy for Steve for finding his passion, I got to hear the rest of his story—his family! He was a father!

That's what can happen when you shift your internal dialogue and ask new questions. What did you enjoy doing when you were a child? What brought you joy when you were a teenager? What did you want to be when you grew up? What dreams have you forgotten about? Here is the kicker: what if you were willing to answer honestly and not worry about what others thought about your answer? Steve transformed his life simply by being willing to ask himself, "What brought me joy when I was young?" and then acting on it.

PLAYBOOK EXERCISE

Discovering Your "Why"

Would you be willing to be present enough to connect with things that brought you joy in the past? What if you shared your answer with your family and friends? Imagine what transformations could occur in your life as you find a clearer "why"!

Take a moment and write down answers to three simple questions; be as truthful as you can!

1. What things did you love to do when you were young that you no longer do?
2. What did you want to be when you grew up?
3. What were some of the dreams you had as a child and a teenager?

CHAPTER 6
Rules of the Road

POP! PURPOSE OVER PROCESS

When we are driving somewhere, we are changing our position in two ways: We are driving away from something and toward something else—going from point A to point B. In the same manner, two guiding forces direct everything we do in life: we are avoiding something (typically something painful) and at the same time, we are striving for something else, something that gives us pleasure.

Do you remember *Alice in Wonderland*? Alice falls through the rabbit hole, shrinks, grows, and finds herself in the strange land of Wonderland where she encounters strange creatures and flowers that speak, and immediately she starts to panic. She is disoriented, confused, and scared—all non-resourceful States, and we know that decisions made in non-resourceful States are usually bad decisions. Alice is wondering which way to go when she encounters the Cheshire Cat. When the Cheshire Cat asks her where she wants to go, Alice answers, "Well, it really doesn't matter . . . anywhere but here!" The Cheshire Cat then tells her that if she doesn't know *where* she wants to go, then it doesn't really matter *which way* she goes. This is exactly how many of us navigate through life. We don't really know where we want to go but we get behind the wheel of our car anyway and start out—often in a bad State. Now we're on the open road without a destination in our Emotional Guidance System (EGS) and probably without adequate or the proper type of fuel. Remember that bad fuel equals a bad State.

How many times have you "done an Alice" and made a decision based on simply wanting to get out of somewhere without knowing where you really wanted to be? When Alice did it, it wasn't very effective for her and it won't be very effective for you, either. The things that drive us are needs, and the desire to "get out of here"—wherever "here" may be at the time—is a need. But these types of needs or desires are not well-planned or thought-out. However, there are things that act like thought processes, that guide us and keep us on the road. For instance, double yellow lines—why don't you cross them? *Because you can crash.* You obey the rules and keep double yellow lines on your left not your right because they are there to keep you safe, so that you and your car make it to your destination in one piece. You may want to get out of here, but you need to have a plan—you need a destination in your EGS and you need to follow the rules of the road to get there safely. Some people have a defined purpose—they know exactly where they want to go, which means they can devise an effective plan to get there.

The Happiness Formula

Most people not only don't know where they *want* to go, they only know where they *don't* want to go—what they are trying to avoid. Life can feel like a mystery—we're not born with a manual on how to live our lives or how to achieve happiness, so we spend a great deal of time looking for it and the key to success. Can you imagine how much time and effort we could save if we had a formula to follow? What if I told that there is, in fact, a formula for happiness? Here it is:

Happiness: LC = BP

LC stands for Life Conditions—the conditions of your life *right now*—which include where you live, your emotional, spiritual, and financial States, and what terms you're on with your friends and family. BP stands for your blueprint—the plan or model of what your life *should* look like—which includes your system of beliefs, values, and the rules that you live by. *I'm okay with this... but not that.*

Right now, there are parts of your life that you're okay with and parts that you are not okay with. If there weren't parts of your life that you would like to change, you wouldn't be reading this book. (We already established that drugs and alcohol were originally not a problem—they were a solution to those things that you weren't okay with, the things you would like to change.)

Let's do a little exercise. Get a pen and a piece of paper—I'll wait... Ready? Okay, think of the parts of your life that you *are* okay with and write those things down. Now look your list. Do your life conditions for those things equal your expectations, blueprint, or general idea of how life should be? They should, and for those things LC = BP, so you should at least be content, if not happy.

Now, make a list of things in your life that you are *not* okay with. Do they cause you stress, frustration, or pain? Notice that on this list, your LC does not equal your BP or your expectations: LC ≠ BP!

Let's use addiction treatment as an example. I'm going to go out on a limb and guess that in high school, you spoke about your future and maybe even sat with your guidance counselor to talk about your life plans. Perhaps you said, "I'm going to college" or "I'd like to start a business." You may even have aspired to become a doctor, mechanic, musician, actress, or astronaut, but I'm pretty sure you didn't say, "You know what would be really cool? If I struggle with addiction and go to rehab!" No one plans to go down that road, so when you got there you thought, *Daaaamn!* Because it's *not in your blueprint!* You're not thrilled to be there. It doesn't make you happy. As a matter of fact, it probably caused you a great deal of discomfort or pain, but you went anyway hoping to overcome those feelings.

What about your family? I'm sure your parents held you in their arms as a baby and dreamt of a great life for you. They didn't take a look at how wonderful you were and think, *Wow, if only you could struggle with addition and go to rehab!* No, they're feeling pain and discomfort because they had a certain blueprint of the type of life they wanted you to have. Maybe they even blame themselves for the way things turned out. It's the same with your partner or significant other—they all had a blueprint or expectation of how their lives would play out standing by your side.

Now, when your LC ≠ BP, what do you have to change to be happy? *You have to change one of the two sides to balance the equation.*

PLAYBOOK EXERCISE

WHEEL OF LIFE

- Intrapersonal 10
- Finance 10
- Profession/Career/Mission 10
- Intrapersonal 10
- Spirituality 10
- Social 10
- Time Management 10
- Health/Physiology 10
- Family 10
- Fun 10

The Wheel of Life is made up of 10 components. What stops you from being a 10 in each area?

Finance _____

Profession _____

Spirit _____

Health _____

Fun _____

Family _____

Time _____

Social _____

Interpersonal _____

Intrapersonal _____

Have you ever been in a relationship where things start to get a little sour and you end the relationship? You move on and find someone new, only to find that you're in the same relationship you just got out of but with someone else. Or maybe you had a job and you weren't happy so you found a new job. Before long, you start to feel the same emotions you felt in your previous job—the same problems arise and you realize that you're in a new job with the same old nemesis... the only thing that changed was the face. That happens when you only change your LC. To *really* transform, you have to update your BP. You have to update your beliefs, values, rules, and strategies to make a lasting change.

Think back to when you were actively using drugs or alcohol. How quickly could you find your drug of choice? What if you were dropped off in the middle of nowhere with very few resources. How quickly could you find your DOC? Pretty quickly, right? That's because your blueprint is wired for it. Regardless of your life conditions at that moment, your blueprint and all your rules and strategies make you extremely resourceful at finding what you need in little or no time. To make change, *you have to change your blueprint*. Only when your substance of choice is no longer of value to you will your life conditions align and make the equation true.

Updating Your Blueprint

When you actively change both your blueprint and your life conditions, *you speed the process up exponentially!* This is where lasting change happens. This is where you experience a true shift in your life. If you go through treatment and change your blueprint a little bit but your life conditions are still the same, you will likely go back to your old patterns. And if your family doesn't change with you,

you're pretty likely to fall back. They have to change their blueprint, too, so that they don't continue to treat you the same as they used to, which could put you right back where you were before treatment. If the people you love treat you like an unreliable addict, then you are prone to act like an unreliable addict. I highly encourage engaging in a family program so that everyone has an opportunity to change their blueprint. "Home" is an emotionally challenging front after you've been through rehab, even if you don't go there immediately. Some people say that changing the location of your home is key, but sometimes you can't change it, so first you have to change your attitude. You have to evaluate where you are going after recovery—update your BP and update your LC—then, encourage your loved ones to do the same.

We've just talked about the emotions that you do the most to avoid, now let's talk about the emotions that you do the most to experience. You're going to need a pen and a piece of paper again ... Ready? Okay, think about the things you want to avoid and write them down. Then think about where you want to go in life—things you want to experience—and write them down. It was easier to come up with emotions or States that you want to avoid than to come up with things you want to experience, right? That's because you're wired that way as a human being. You're wired to avoid pain at all cost, so your brain is geared to recognize anything that could be painful or negative. You're constantly asking yourself things such as, *How did I get screwed?* And, *how did I let this happen again?* If you're constantly looking for what is wrong, you will constantly find it. "Seek and you shall find." Ask crappy questions and you'll get crappy answers.

Often when we are asked to think of what we want, we instead think of what we *don't* want, which isn't very effective. Now, if I ask you not to think of the purple elephant in the room, the first thing you will visualize is the purple elephant because our brains don't recognize negatives. But, thinking of what you do *not* want is as effective as driving your car by looking in your rearview mirror. You're looking back at an accident and your thoughts are telling you that you don't want to crash and burn, too, but you're so busy looking backward instead of forward that you actually end up crashing and burning.

We do this interesting thing with time; we have these temporal dynamics that we play with. We're either living in the past or we're living in the future. We're either going "if this had never happened back then, this other thing wouldn't have happened." We bring all this stuff up and experience it now but it didn't happen now. *It's all in the past—we're looking through our rearview mirror!* Or we're worrying about something that might happen down the road, only it never even happens. We're not being present.

Can you experience being present on the phone? Sure. You're physically in a different place but you can still be present. That means you're not bringing up the past and all the problems and the pain, because your loved one already knows the pain they've caused and they feel like shit about it. Let's say that someone you know intimately feels worthless because of the guilt and the shame and the pain that they've caused you and that's all they're focusing on—they just feel like crap. Do you think they're going to tap into more or less potential or power? Less, of course. And what about the results? They're going to disappoint you again because they're disappointed in themselves, and they think, *See? I told you so. I'm worthless. I cause so much pain!* And it's only because someone brought up pain from the past instead of being present. Think about fear—when you are feeling fearful, it's because of something you're creating in the future—it hasn't even happened! You're not present, you're temporally not here, you're somewhere else. You've gone either into the past or into the future and distorted or generalized a situation that already happened or hasn't happened and you're feeling the pain of something that is nonexistent. If you happen to be on the receiving end of that conversation, you think, *What the hell? I feel so bad right now!* It's because someone just poured a big, stinking pile of crap into the conversation.

The emotions or States that you habitually live in or focus on will only be magnified by the circumstances of your life. For example, people think they want money—they actually think that money will make them happy, but money simply enhances the strength of the fuel in their engine. Remember what fuel is? It's your State. If you're an angry person and you get money, you'll just be an angry rich person. It won't make you a happy rich person because you will find reasons to still be angry. Maybe you'll be angry thinking of all the people who want a chunk of your money, or maybe you'll be angry when you lose some of that money on a bad investment. Money doesn't change your State, it just makes you more pissed off, more bitter, more resentful. The only way to be truly happy is to generate your own happiness, then even poor circumstances can't take it away.

Let's go back to the list of States that you want to experience. Even if two people have the same list of States, they will likely place them in different order based on importance. And consider this: words may have different connotations for different people. For example, the phrase "at ease" and the word "peaceful" may mean the same thing to one person while having a completely different meaning to another person. Why? Because they have different blueprints!

PLAYBOOK EXERCISE

Experiencing and Avoiding States

Take the five primary emotions or States that you do the most to *experience* and rank them in order of importance. These are the emotions that bring you pleasure and relieve pain. Some examples include: excitement, freedom, pride, passion, and love. If you run into trouble, take two States at a time and ask yourself, "In the past, did I do more to experience *this* emotion or *that* emotion?" Repeat the process until you have ranked them all from most important to least important.

Now, take the five primary emotions or States that you do the most to *avoid* and rank them in the same manner (awareness is key)! Once you've done that, go back to the list of emotions that you want to *experience* and pair them with the list you made of the ones you want to *avoid*. Your list should look something like this when you are done:

Frustration >>> Relaxation

Fear >>> Safety

Anger >>> Love

Loss >>> Release

Stress >>> Happiness

Who Makes the Rules?

Now that you see the hierarchy or ranking of emotions that you'd do the most to experience and the ones you'd do the most to avoid, think about how they compare to lists made by other people. Do you think they are the same? Doubtful. People have different emotions and States that they want to experience or avoid and even when there are similarities or overlaps, they will be ranked differently according to that individual's blueprint. Individuals are fascinating—every head is a world of its own.

The reason we have conflicts with others is because we have different models of the world yet we still assume they think the way we do. That means, when people differ from us, we experience conflict. Has anyone ever said to you, "How could you do this to me?" Well, did you do anything to them? Perhaps you don't feel that you did, you were just going about your business according to your rules or your blueprint that didn't align with theirs and now they feel injured. When you put your blueprint on someone else, guess what happens? *Stress happens!*

Finish this sentence: Rules are meant to be . . .? No, they're meant to be *followed*. But whose rules do you follow? *Your rules*. Remember the double yellow lines scenario—the lines that separate traffic heading in one direction from traffic heading in another direction? That is a rule. If you violate that rule, you will crash. Likewise, all pain and all anger are nothing more than "rules violations." Someone crossed your double yellow lines and drove into your traffic. When other people don't follow your rules, you get mad, and when you don't follow their rules, they get mad. That's because we assume that everyone else thinks just like we do—we assume everyone else has the same blueprint that we do. The catch is that *they assume the same thing!* They aren't deliberately breaking your rules, they are simply following their own rules or putting theirs before yours. According to their world model, they haven't done anything wrong, they are just following rules as well.

Have you ever given much thought to the conditions or rules that need to be present in order for you to feel either negative or positive emotions? The playbook exercise you just did should give you some insight into those rules. Look at your list and answer truthfully—are the conditions that make you feel negative emotions easier to achieve than those that make you feel positive emotions? Do your positive emotions depend heavily on outside influences? Could they be a bit codependent?

Most of us have conditions that make it nearly impossible—or at least improbable—for us to sustain positive emotions. That is perhaps one of the reasons why we use drugs and alcohol—they help us to connect with emotions and feelings in an artificial way.

Now you know that those conditions are nothing more than rules. And whose rules are they? *Yours!* They are written in your blueprint, but *you* own your blueprint. You have every right and the power to update it whenever you want. You don't require someone or something else in order to feel good—*all you need is you!*

Right now, the way your blueprint is written makes it difficult to feel pleasure and easy to feel pain. It's time to update your blueprint so that it's easy to feel pleasure and difficult to feel pain. The reason you feel upset, angry, or frustrated is that you are forgetting something in the moment. You are experiencing negative emotions because you are forgetting that you are great, that you are strong.

You need to discover who you are—what fits into your rules. Finish the following sentence based on your rules and your blueprint: To feel at ease and safe I have to remember that I am...?

PLAYBOOK EXERCISE

Shift Your Blueprint

Read the two questions below, then write down your thoughts. These questions will help you discover new rules and shift your blueprint, making it easier for you to experience pleasure and more difficult for you to experience pain.

1. What are you forgetting about yourself in order to feel pain?

   _____

   _____

2. What do you need to remember about yourself in order to feel pleasure?

   _____

   _____

BACK ON THE ROAD

Going forward, you'll have to take on the question, "What am I going to do with the rest of my life?" and in order to answer that, you're going to ask yourself even more questions like, "How do I live now without using?" and "Where do I start?" Rarely (if ever) do we ask just one question that has one simple answer—questions are stacked, and stacked frantically. Now these new questions will inevitably involve other parts of your life, which could be very disheartening to most people as uncertainty peeks its head around every bend along the roadway. This frantic stacking of questions, by the way, is how we "do" the State of "overwhelm." We create that state by thinking of lots of things at once while asking open-ended "what if" questions that have no definitive answers, and focusing on all the things that won't work at the same time. We say things that don't support to our goals, such as, "this is too much for me," and "I just can't keep up," or we ask disempowering questions like, "Why does this always happen to me?" and "Why can't I quit?" When you allow yourself to become overwhelmed and confused and find yourself in that non-resourceful state, you will either be unable to make any decisions at all or, worse, you will make poor ones. But you're equipped to handle multiple questions and challenges now because you know how to approach big questions and stressful situations. And you also know to ask yourself valuable questions because shallow questions will only produce shallow answers, or as we've said throughout this book, crappy questions will yield crappy answers.

So, what do you do? *(You know this!)* Right... change your State! And how do you do that? Change your physiology (pick your head up and get into a more positive physical position); adjust your EGS and update your map—your personal blueprint; kick your RAS into gear (where focus goes, energy flows); make sure that your BS (Belief System) equals your LC (Life Conditions); and always remember that nothing has any meaning except the meaning you give it—be careful how you label things, *you will believe anything that you tell yourself!*

Start every single day by filling up with top-grade fuel—dance, sing, do whatever it takes to produce a quality State. Now, top off your super car, clean the windshield, get out on the road, and enjoy the detours; they are the situations and adventures that bring change.

True Story: Manifestation Proxy

A few years ago, my mother remarried. Her new husband was—and still is—a wonderful, caring, and loving man. What he wasn't—and still isn't—is healthy; he never took very good care of himself. He neither treated his body like a temple nor a Tesla. In other words, he didn't maintain his vehicle well at all and took the path of least resistance when it came to fueling up and maintenance, i.e., health and wellness.

Just before their wedding, my stepfather began having some health issues (if I remember correctly, it was some form of pancreatitis or pancreatic cancer). One thing I remember with certainty, however, was how he cared for himself after his diagnoses. He went on a quest to find a magic pill that would restore his health, and he sought the easiest and most convenient things available to help him cure the symptoms.

It's probably important to tell you at this point that both my mother and he smoked and drank. Neither one of them took very good care of themselves.

I'm going to back up a bit now and share a little of my mother's behavior as I was growing up. As far back as I can remember, she was an extraordinarily loving woman who always tried to be as helpful and supportive as possible, especially to those she loved. She had a variety of interesting friends and they spent lots of time together, to the point that they were a constant part of my home environment. As my brother and I got older, we spent a considerable amount of time on our own while my mother would bring struggling people into our home. At times it felt almost as though she was taking in stray animals—in fact, when I was about sixteen years of age, she took in one of my own friends who was struggling with familial challenges at home.

I recall a particular life lesson that my mother learned from her mother, which made a great impression on me. She would often say that it is our *duty* to take care of those less fortunate than ourselves. It's a lesson that is perfectly congruent with my mother's own childhood because she was adopted. My grandmother spent her life taking care of unfortunates, too.

But, back to my mother's planned nuptials... Vividly I recall the day of her wedding as she experienced a mild breakdown over concerns about her fiancée's lack of self-care. Emphatically she told me, "I do not want to be a caretaker! I do not want to be a caretaker! *I do not want to be a caretaker!*"

Here's a little scenario that illustrates perfectly the predicament my mother was in: A man is driving in the desert with nothing in sight other than the light posts lining the road every 100 yards or so. Somehow, the car crashes into one of the 12-inch-wide light posts. With all that open road, how did he end up crashing into a light post even though there were giant gaps between them? Here's how: When he started to lose control, he was focused solely on *not* hitting the light post and probably thinking, "I hope I don't hit that light post! I hope I don't hit that light post!" While his desire was to *avoid* hitting the light post, the fact that his focus was *on* the light post and his last three words were "hit the light post," it manifested as the very thing he was focusing on, which was the light post.

Now, going back to my mother's wedding and her comment to me that she did *not* want to be a caretaker—notice that her last three words were "be a caretaker," Just take a look at quantum physics for a simple model showing how a manifestation proxy occurs when your focus is on what you *don't want* instead of visualizing what you *do want*. (But if you do the work—the rehab—you can train yourself to change your focus!)

As time went on and her marriage to this wonderful man continued, he continued with less than ideal health strategies. At first, his unhealthy lifestyle did not impact their lives much at all, but after a few years, when they decided that it was time to retire, his carefree lifestyle cast its shadow. My stepfather worked diligently throughout his life to create financial abundance, and now it was time to enjoy that abundance. But he neglected to maintain his car and it wasn't long before he was in the shop and facing open heart surgery. What do you think his doctors told him about smoking? Of course...they said, *"No smoking!"* Initially, my stepfather attempted (rather painfully) to comply. I remember witnessing his struggle and asking him, "How would you describe your relationship with smoking?" He said, "I am a smoker and when I turn seventy-five, I am going to start smoking again!" But even before the year was out, he was smoking. To make matters worse, he was not willing to do the physical rehab recommended by his doctors and that old lifestyle pattern that sparked my mother's fear of being a caretaker was evident once again. He was simply unwilling to do what was necessary to maintain a healthy, vibrant life.

Not long after the bypass experience, my mother and stepfather went on a dream cruise in the Baltic Sea on a superbly elegant ship with less than 100 people on board. It was a wonderful, exclusive opportunity to enjoy the best the world had to offer, and it was during that exquisite cruise that my stepfather suffered a stroke and spent the following month recovering in a hospital in Greece. The stroke caused some loss in the use of his right side, but he was still able to walk and function fairly well. It also caused mild aphasia, an impairment of language skills that affects the production or comprehension of speech, including the ability to read and write. As you can imagine, the effects of the stroke created extraordinary stress for my mother and my stepfather. At the hospital in Greece, what advice do you think the doctors gave him after the stroke? Exactly... *"Stop smoking!"* But when they finally got home from that frightening experience, adamantly he stated once more, "When I turn seventy-five I'm going to start smoking again!" And once again, within the year, he was doing just that.

Although my stepfather was able to walk to some degree, the stroke left him unable to drive, which meant that my mother was responsible for all the driving, making him totally dependent on her. And just as he was in previous challenges, he was less than willing to do the rehab work that would help him develop a healthier life. Things did not improve.

For a minute, let's take a look at his situation from the perspective of a car. What happens to the rubber tubing, gaskets, and such when you just let a car sit? They dry up and fall apart, don't they?

What do you think happens to our bodies when we do the same thing—when we sit around and neglect to engage them? The same thing happens—we start to slow down and can't function as well as we used to. Well, over the next few years my stepfather suffered even more strokes and unexplained seizures and each time he refused to do the rehab work that would improve his health. At first, he said it was uncomfortable and then it became painful. Eventually, he lost almost all use of the right side of his body and a more extreme aphasia affected him to the extent that his vocabulary consisted of only four words: yes, no, right, and fuck you. And due to his lack of mobility, he could no longer smoke without someone's help, but since no one would help him, he quit by proxy. My stepfather was so mired in the identity of being "a smoker" that he couldn't help but smoke. Why? *Because smokers smoke.* That is what they do.

Eventually, my stepfather was tested to see what type of permanent brain damage was causing his lack of mobility. What the doctors discovered was not extraordinary by any means—he was experiencing *atrophy*. Because he was unwilling to do speech and muscle therapy, he was experiencing acute atrophy that affected his limbs and his ability to speak. The rubber tubing and gaskets in his Tesla dried up and fell apart.

No doubt you can guess how the story played out for my loving, caring mother. She became a caretaker—the one thing she did not want to be.

Dug and Heidi McGuirk are the founders of Revolutionary Growth, an organization that helps people learn how to use their drive and desire to become powerful role models, convert anger and frustration into love and passion, transmute fear into faith, and leave a Rockstar Legacy.

At Revolutionary Growth, their greatest passion is to help people achieve their full potential and live their dreams. Dug and Heidi's training and experience have given them keen insights and skills to help their clients "Feed their Passion, and Starve their Fear" by helping them discover the miracle they already are and always were. Their passion and enthusiasm are exceeded only by their genuine care and desire to honor others' personal journeys.

Revolutionary Growth is a one-stop-shop for anything human in the context of personal development, integrating Mind, Body and Spirit. Dug and Heidi call it *Trans-Lightenment!*

Praise for Dug McGuirk

Dug consistently positions himself strategically along the path of success for his multitude of clients. He helps them understand where they are, how to get to where they want to be and what is required to get there. He then empowers them with the right tools and support to make their vision a reality.

—**Adam Bricker**, television producer

Dug has the unique ability to deliver psychological information in a way that is informative, easy to understand, and entertaining. His message is both memorable and applicable to anyone who is fortunate enough to attend one of his presentations.

—**Patty French**, Association of Professional Flight Attendants

About Dug McGuirk

Dug McGuirk (Delray Beach, FL) is an accomplished entrepreneur, musician, producer and inspirational speaker. He ran his own production company for ten years, contributing to the sale of over 150 million records and multiple Grammys for his clients. Dug was a partner in an international hardware and software computer company and toured the United States as a musician and a top speaker/trainer for Tony Robbins. He was a contributing author in the book *Multiple Streams of Inspiration*. Dug is also a Master Practitioner and Trainer of NLP (neurolinguistic programming) and certified in Neo-Ericsonian Hypnosis. Overcoming a serious drug and alcohol problem early in life enabled Dug to become well versed in true-life experiences and overcome personal obstacles to achieve success. You can contact him at *Dug@RevolutionaryGrowth.com*

Feed your Passion. Starve your Fear
www.revolutionarygrowth.com